BFI Modern Classics

Rob White
Series Editor

BFI Modern Classics is a series of critical studies of films produced over the last three decades. Writers explore their chosen films, offering a range of perspectives on the dominant art and entertainment medium in contemporary culture. The series gathers together snapshots of our passion for and understanding of recent movies.

Also Published

Dilwale Dulhania Le Jayenge
Anupama Chopra

Jaws
Antonia Quirke

Eyes Wide Shut
Michel Chion

Heat
Nick James

(see a full list of titles in the series at the back of this book)

A City of Sadness
悲情城市

Bérénice Reynaud

 Publishing

First published in 2002 by the
British Film Institute
21 Stephen Street, London W1T 1LN

Copyright © Bérénice Reynaud 2002

The British Film Institute promotes greater
understanding and appreciation of,
and access to, film and moving image
culture in the UK.

British Library Cataloguing-in-Publication Data
A catalogue record for this book is available
from the British Library

ISBN 0-85170-930-3

Series design by Andrew Barron &
Collis Clements Associates

Typeset in Italian Garamond and Swiss 721BT
by D R Bungay Associates, Burghfield, Berks

Printed in Great Britain by
Cromwell Press, Trowbridge, Wiltshire

Contents

Acknowledgments

This book is dedicated to Counsellor Jeff Yao, a priceless gem.

Invaluable research assistance was provided by my students and former students An Je-yi, Chen Jo-fei, Chuang Wen-yao, Carol Tsui Lyn Ho, Tom Lin Shu Yu, Motoko Honda and by film-maker Mei-juin Chen.

Special thanks to my editor, Rob White, for his patience and support; to Thom Andersen, Olivier Assayas, Chris Berry, Peggy Chiao Hsiung-ping, Chiu Fu-sheng, Bernard Eisenschitz, Sophie Gluck, Ray Jiing, Huang Li-ming, Huang Yu-chang, Vivian Huang, Bono Lau, Cheng-Sim Lim, Jacques Picoux, Barbara Robinson, Jonathan Rosenbaum, Shu Kei, Christophe Tsen, Norman Wang, Wang Shau-di, Paul Willemen, the staff of 3H Films Ltd (especially Joyce Chen), the Taiwanese Government Information Office (GIO), the Taiwan Film Centre, the faculty, students and staff of the Taiwan National College of Arts, the research staff of the Taipei Cinematheque, Les Films de l'Atalante, as well as to Hou Hsiao-hsien, Chu Tien-wen and Wu Nien-jen, who graciously gave me their time and wonderful interviews.

And to JP, always.

Note on Chinese Names

Two systems compete for the Romanisation of Chinese proper names: the Wade–Giles system, still in use in Taiwan and in the Western world till the mid-1980s, and the *pinyin*, used in Mainland China and in Western academic circles in the last 20 years. Hou Hsiao-hsien is the Wade–Giles transcription, and Hou Xiaoxian the *pinyin*.

In this book, I have used the Wade–Giles system for all Taiwanese proper names, including that of political leaders and parties such as Chiang Kai-shek (instead of Jiang Jieshi in *pinyin*) and Kuomintang (instead of Guomindang) and geographical names such as Taipei (instead of Taibei) – and the *pinyin* for everything else. In the filmography, the Chinese titles are in *pinyin*.

Traditional Chinese names put the family name first (Hou, Chu), and the given name (Hsiao-hsien, Tien-wen) second. However, in the case of people who prefer an English name, I have followed the common Western use: Edward Yang, Tony Leung. In scholarly texts, the practice is often to follow this new 'Westernised' name by the original given name in Chinese: Edward Yang Dechang. I have not done so here, except in the case of Tony Leung Chiu-wai, to differentiate him from his namesake, the actor Tony Leung Ka-fai.

1 Chinese History Is Made at Night

In Beijing, during the night of 4 June 1989, the troops of the People's Liberation Army (PLA) entered Tiananmen Square, broadcasting an order for the students gathered there to evacuate. By 5.40 am, the square was cleared. Killing continued in the streets throughout the morning. This was followed by an intense crackdown on the democracy movement. A few months later, on 15 September, *A City of Sadness,* by the Taiwanese director Hou Hsiao-hsien, was awarded the Golden Lion at the 46th Venice International Film Festival – one of the first contemporary Chinese movies to receive such a prestigious international prize[1] Yet, in December, at Taipei's Golden Horse Awards, *A City of Sadness* lost out to a Hong Kong film, Stanley Kwan's *Full Moon in New York*[2] – a shock to many, considering the upsurge of national pride generated by the Venice award and the tremendous box-office success achieved by the film in Taiwan. Made possible by the 1987 lifting of a 40-year-old martial law, *A City of Sadness* was released in the sorrowful aftermath of the 4 June incident and greeted with suspicion by the Taiwanese establishment. It is a film haunted by the intricacies of recent Chinese history.

Born in 1947 in the mainland province of Guangdong, Hou Hsiao-hsien had lived in Taiwan since infancy, and, while totally Chinese, his film had a distinct Taiwanese flavour and atmosphere and created a world quite different from the 'China' that Western audiences had been introduced to by Fifth Generation mainland film-makers such as Zhang Yimou and Chen Kaige. The 'sadness' of the title alluded to the troubled years between the end of the Japanese occupation of Taiwan in 1945 and the official takeover by the Nationalist Party (Kuomintang) of Chiang Kai-shek in 1949. Yet this 'sadness' has even more distant causes – the division of China and Taiwan's progressive alienation from the mainland since the nineteenth century. And, as fate would have it, *A City of Sadness* reached the world at a moment when, once again, the Chinese psyche was hurting. As he was working on the editing in the spring and summer of 1989, Hou 'immediately sensed the connection between Tiananmen and the massacres alluded to in the film, wondering "Why do such tragedies keep

Soldiers taking Wen-ching to court

befalling the Chinese people?" and hoping that his film would evoke the same pain and anger in its audience'.[3] So, while it is because of its *mise en scène* that *A City of Sadness* has been hailed as 'one of the supreme masterworks of the contemporary cinema',[4] the role played by the historical context in the conception and reception of the film should not be overlooked.

To recreate a portion of Taiwanese history that until then had been shrouded in darkness, Hou follows, then subverts, the genre of the 'family saga', recounting the intertwining lives of an extended family in a small town on the northern coast of Taiwan: four brothers, their relatives, associates and friends. They become victims of the increasing violence that befalls the island. His ninth feature,[5] *A City of Sadness* was an aesthetic breakthrough for Hou – not only did he use sync sound for the first time (becoming the first Taiwanese film-maker to do so), but he combined his characteristic long shots with a more atmospheric, less linear type of montage. Through his minimalist imagery, complex framing, elliptic rendering of interpersonal relationships, and the disruptions created by his storytelling techniques (breaks in continuity editing, flashbacks-within-flashbacks), Hou involves the spectator emotionally, while leaving him or her intellectually responsible for reconstructing the multiple layers of the plot.

Hou describes how he structured the story with his screenwriters, Chu Tien-wen and Wu Nien-jen:

We laid the basis [of the narrative structure] by reconstructing the feelings and emotions of that time ... creating an atmosphere ... therefore producing a subjective view towards this whole period of time … Then they built up the characters, and depending on their importance, they poured details gathered through their historical research into them – then re-started all over again … Since so many things happen in the background, we'd rather use flashbacks than a linear structure, and introduce [the spectator to the story] through a multiplicity of details. In the editing process, it became unimportant to define what was reality and what was flashback; I like to blur the line between the two.[6]

Already present in Hou's earlier films, this 'subjective view' of history can be defined as a form of Impressionism[7] – but never had it been brought to such a level of shimmering complexity as in *A City*, due to the number of the characters involved, the length of the film (159 minutes) and the poignant historical significance of the events recounted. Overall, *A City* defines a vertiginous, elliptical arc, which goes from one feeling of loss – the loss of Taiwan by the Japanese – to another – the loss of the mainland by the Kuomintang.

Weaving History with Multiple Threads

It is on the voice of a broken, yet mythical Japanese man, that Hou starts *A City of Sadness*. On 15 August 1945, Emperor Hirohito spoke directly to his people for the first time. He used a modern medium, the radio, while uttering a language that most of his subjects could not understand: classical Japanese. The bombings of Hiroshima and Nagasaki had forced him to concede defeat. His voice resonated through all Japanese territories and possessions, as far as the small, distant island of Taiwan. As the credits roll, we hear his speech and it continues over a few seconds of black frames, then is heard in the warm chiaroscuro of a private house. A middle-aged, heavy-set man, Lin Wen-heung, lights incense with the flames of two candles, smoking and looking worried. In the background, one perceives the shady presence of another man, Ah-ga, the brother of Wen-heung's mistress. As suggested by the off-screen muffled cries of a woman, a baby is about to be born. In another room, the expectant mother is lying on a bed, surrounded by a young nurse and an older midwife, who speaks to her in a gentle but firm tone. A third cut brings back Wen-heung, this time facing us; in the background, the midwife appears like a 'Chinese shadow' behind a red-pink curtain. The nurse is already out of the room, announcing she's going to get some warm water. After the two women have left the field, a panning shot follows Wen-heung, who joins them as they are scooping hot water, and tells them, helplessly but curtly, to 'hurry'. The nurse's body is seen as a silhouette against a window, while the midwife is kept in the dark.

Wen-heung returns to his previous spot, on the right of the screen, and drinks out of a little white teacup, while, suddenly, on his right, a ceiling lamp lights up. 'Fuck, now it's coming,' says Wen-heung – alluding both to the return of the electricity, often cut during wartime, and to the arrival of the baby. He pulls up the cloth that had been put over the bulb, undoubtedly to avoid attracting attention in the event of an air-raid. Hirohito's voice has gradually grown weaker and weaker, while the woman's moaning suddenly becomes louder. A few seconds later, Hirohito has completely vanished and is replaced by the theme music. Wen-heung goes to the bedroom on the right, leaving the frame empty. A big cry is heard, then the voice of the midwife: 'It's a boy. Congratulations!' On the image, Chinese titles appear, then their translation in English:

August 15, 1945.
The Japanese Emperor announced unconditional surrender.
Taiwan was free after 51 years of Japanese rule.
Lin Wen-heung's woman in Badouzi bore him a son.
They named him Lin Kang-ming ('Light').

After the disappearance of the titles, the camera stays on the empty field, lit on the right with the hanging bulb, in the centre by a lone, flickering candle and on the left by the window, through which we can barely discern the first light of dawn. The low droning gives way to the film's musical theme, then, over black frames, the title appears. The next cut shows the long shot of a landscape still drowned in darkness.

In this masterful opening sequence – lasting a little over four minutes – Hou introduces the diegetic and formal themes of the film. First, he elegantly weaves the notion of an extended Chinese family into the narrative structure, presenting Wen-heung's relationship with his mistress (unnamed in the rest of the story) and second family as the casual, common occurrence it was in Chinese society at the time.[8] His wife (Mio), children and 'first' family never allude to the relationship, and we see Wen-heung commuting between the Lin family home, his concubine's house and his business without much fuss. From the onset, Hou anchors the fiction in the body language of Chen Sown-yung (who plays Wen-heung, the 'Big Brother' of the Lin family, and the expectant dad), a film and TV actor well-known to Taiwanese spectators. Even Western audiences cannot fail to relate to Chen's powerful physical presence, his arresting mixture of masterly impatience and childish greediness (later in the film, Mio scolds him for

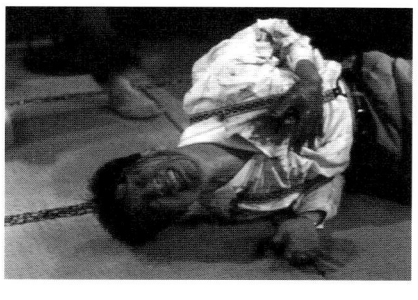

Ah-ga attacked by the Shanghaiese gangsters

drinking, again, out of a teapot) – of imperial command of the space and sloppiness (we hear his sandals dragging on the floor as he goes to speak to the nurse and midwife) – of 'manly' chain-smoking and helplessness when faced with the mysteries of the female body.

Second, Hou sets up a series of formal and dramatic tensions that outlines the parameters of the narrative structure. On the soundtrack the main opposition is between the voice of history (here represented by Hirohito) and the voices coming from this private, intimate sphere that are, in Hou's films as well, usually *entrusted to women*. However, since *A City* unfolds a polyphony of accents, dialects and utterances, it presents a more complex reality than a mere male/female counterpoint. At the level of the image, a major source of tension – and dynamism – is the constant interplay between emptiness and fullness, darkness and colour, light and darkness – how light is born out of the dark, colour out of the black and the void out of things themselves. These tensions spring, on the one hand, from Hou's aesthetic choices as they have been informed by Chinese and Japanese traditions and, on the other, from the opposition the film is drawing between the warmth of family life and the harshness of historical events. Later, Wen-heung will accurately describe the place and time the protagonists live in: 'How pitiful we are living on this island! First it is the Japanese, then the Chinese. Eaten by everyone, ridden by everyone, sympathized by no-one.'[9]

Taiwan's 'tragedy' lies in its uneasy relationship with the mainland, defined from the onset by fascination, hope, exile, invasion, civil war and estrangement. A small but lush island off the south-east coast of China, facing Fujian province, Taiwan was originally populated with South Pacific (Malay) aborigines. In the fifteenth century, Chinese immigration started, composed mainly of Hakka (a population of immigrants from the north, speaking their own dialect, which had fled to the provinces of Guangdong and Fujian to escape persecution) and Fujianese (whose dialect, slightly corrupted, became the Taiwanese language). In 1517 Portuguese sailors landed on the island, and called her 'Formosa' ('the beautiful one'). In 1624 the Dutch occupied it, but were ousted by the young general Cheng Chengkun (Koxinga) in 1661. A partisan of the Ming Dynasty, Cheng had been forced to retreat by the Manchu army and was hoping to use Taiwan as a strategic base to regroup his forces. Instead, he died a year later; in 1682, the Manchu captured the island, and turned it into a province of the Middle Empire in 1887.

In 1894, the (in)famous Dowager Empress CiXi started – and lost – a war against Japan and, a year later, signed the treaty of Shimonoseki, which included among its terms the surrender of Taiwan to Japan. In the next 50 years, Taiwan underwent a rigorous occupation. Thousands of Japanese settlers – soldiers, administrators, businessmen – arrived on the island, where they imposed the Japanese language. While mercilessly suppressing any hint of an uprising, the occupying forces attempted to 'Japanise' the inhabitants, forcibly but efficiently developing the economy, spreading literacy through a government-supported school system – thereby creating a situation of colonial hybridity, love–hate and interdependency whose effects are still felt today. Feeling abandoned by a distant Chinese power, many Taiwanese found a new identity in the culture of the occupying forces; Japanese became the *lingua franca* for at least three generations, and elements of Japanese architecture can be found throughout the island.

In the first half-hour of *A City*, Hou delicately suggests the traces left by the Japanese occupation in staging an encounter between the young nurse Hinomi and her Japanese friend Shisuko, as the latter is waiting to be repatriated back to Japan with her elderly father, Mr Ogawa, the former principal of the Japanese school. The episode, which contains the first flashback of the film, is bracketed within two similar shots showing, in a wide angle and from the inside of the building, the entrance of the Miners' Hospital where Hinomi works. As discussed later (see Chapter Four), these images, which recur regularly throughout the film, belong to the category of *visual motif shots*.

At the beginning of the sequence, Shisuko is seen walking through the centre of the hospital gate, carrying a sword and a package wrapped in a saffron cloth; in that space, due to the protruding shape of the sword on both sides of her body, her silhouette suggests the shape of a cross. This striking image marks a sharp contrast with the visual motif shot closing the sequence, in which four men, most of them gangsters, come to the same hospital to visit Wen-leung, the Lin family's third brother, who, drafted into the Japanese army, has had to be hospitalised on his return on account of severe shellshock. The first line Wen-leung's visitors are heard uttering is 'Business is the business of men, isn't it?' On the other hand, the encounter between Hinomi and Shisuko is silent at first, and then unfolds in the hushed tones of gentile propriety and a genuine, yet wounded affection between friends who are about to part for ever. Hou is not merely outlining a contrast between the gentle world of women and the harsher, more violent world of men, for the episode that began with the encounter between Hinomi and Shisuko continues by involving, via flashback and storytelling, three men – Shisuko's dead brother; Hinomi's own brother, the intellectual Hinoe; and another close friend of Hinoe, Wen-ching, the fourth brother of the Lin family. The dialectical – and melancholic – contrast suggested here is between the two faces of the Japanese occupation: its peaceful, refined, civilising aspect, versus the brutal realities of colonial violence, forced conscription, and the vacancy of power that all too often follows the end of colonisation, with its hideous retinue of carpetbaggers, war profiteers and smugglers. Trained as intellectuals and professionals by the Japanese – Hinoe is a schoolteacher, Hinomi a registered nurse – the two siblings are introduced as being impregnated, moulded and seduced by Japanese culture. Their names come from the transcriptions of the Japanese pronunciation of their original Taiwanese names,[10] and they have warm personal relationships with Japanese settlers. Hinomi's first diary entry still keeps the date as 'the 18th day, 11th month, 26th year of the Showa Emperor'. Yet, in a later scene in which the two siblings entertain their friends at home, dinner concludes on a soulful rendering of a song mourning 'September 18', the date in 1931 of the Shenyang Incident, when the Japanese army seized northern China, starting another Sino–Japanese war – which had devastating effects for the Taiwanese population. Many young men were drafted into the Japanese army and may have had to turn their weapons against other Chinese.

After showing Shisuko entering the hospital, without transition Hou cuts to a tighter shot of the two women sitting together on the floor of a room. In hushed tones, with slow ceremonial gestures, Shisuko gives three objects to Hinomi: the sword, her deceased brother's 'most cherished object'; a scroll poem the latter had written in the presence of Hinoe; and finally a precious kimono, tailored in red silk with white flower motifs. The sword and the poem are to be given to Hinoe, while the kimono is for Hinomi, who first makes a polite attempt at resisting such a gift. The camera never moves and keeps a distance, as if to respect the intensity of the emotions and sadness quietly expressed there, as well as the extreme grace with which Shisuko silences her friend's objections: 'In faraway Japan, I will think of how beautiful Hinomi looks in this kimono.' The scene ends in silence, as the two women slightly bow to each other.

The next cut leads to a flashback, with a panning shot from left to right that reveals small children in a classroom, listening to a young woman singing and playing at the piano. The camera passes the body of a man standing, his head 'cut off' by the low framing, then reaches the woman, who we recognise as Shisuko; the panning resumes in the opposite direction, right and up, this time revealing the standing man as Hinoe, looking at Shisuko with an air of thoughtful rapture, suggesting the possibility of romantic feelings on his part. The exchange of gifts between Shisuko and Hinomi thus appears in a different light – it would have been improper for the young Japanese woman to have remitted them to Hinoe in person, but she can safely do so through the intermediary of a female friend, who is the sister of a man for whom she also may have had a silent attraction. The gifts are an allusion to her brother's manhood (the sword) and to his untimely death (the poem). By giving her kimono to Hinomi, Shisuko may also have hoped that her friend would wear it, creating for Hinoe a visual reminder of the woman it used to adorn.

The possibility of an aborted romance is further – albeit discreetly – explored in the continuation of the flashback. As the music plays on, creating a false temporal continuity, Shisuko is seen wearing the red-and-white kimono, sitting on the floor, arranging flowers in a vase and looking off-screen on the left. The object of her gaze appears in the next shot, in which her brother is writing a poem at a desk, with Hinoe looking at him. This is followed by an intertitle in Chinese, Japanese and English stating the last three verses of the poem:

> Fly as you will and go
> I will follow
> So it is with all of us.

As the piano music continues, another disruption of the temporal continuity occurs, as we jump ahead, *after* the meeting between the two women. In a sort of narrative permutation, we still have two men and one woman, but two of the protagonists have changed, the characters are wearing dark clothes (no red kimono) and the atmosphere is sombre (while the previous flashback unfolded against a white, luminous background). Hinomi has given the poem to her brother, while his friend

Wen-ching, the deaf-mute photographer, is present. The narrative substitution suggests the possibility of another hidden romance, this time between Wen-ching and Hinomi, and indeed, after a fade to black, another shot presents us with Hinomi and Wen-ching alone together, devising the mode of communication that will structure a great part of the film. She writes to him on a piece of paper, and the titles appear on the black screen, as if in a silent movie. She tells him the story of the suicide of a young Japanese woman, who would rather die than 'face the imminent loss of her splendid youth … This was during the Meiji restoration, an era full of enthusiasm and heroic spirit.' At the end of her story, the first line of the poem written by Shisuko's brother is revealed: 'Cherry blossoms, sharing the same fate … '

Poetry, flowers, the lure of death, the hope of a magnificent, heroic, radiant Asian modernity: Hou shows the fascination exerted by Japanese culture over young Chinese intellectuals. CiXi had suppressed any attempts at reform presented to her, and the bankrupted, humiliated Middle Empire had experienced modernity as an ambiguous gift from the Western invaders; conversely, the Meiji restoration (1868–1912) had managed to propel Japan toward modernisation while retaining the essential aspects of its society and culture, therefore avoiding 'contamination' by the West.[11] In the early twentieth century, larger and larger numbers of young Chinese went to study in Japan, in situations that became progressively more tense as Japan was showing imperialist designs over China and racist prejudices towards the Chinese.

In 1911, the Qing Dynasty was toppled and the Republic of China was founded. However, in 1912, Sun Yat-Sen, who had been elected provisional president, was replaced by a military leader, Yuan Shikai, and years of civil war, bloody repression and civil disorder were to follow. In 1924, there was a first United Front between the Kuomintang and the Communist Party (founded in 1921), but, in April 1927, in Shanghai, Chiang Kai-shek ordered the massacre of Communists and union organisers. In September, Mao Zedong withdrew his troops to a mountainous region in the Jianxi province – from which the legendary Long March started in 1934. Against this backdrop, life in occupied

Taiwan was a model of peace and order. However, since 1914, both in Taiwan and among young Taiwanese studying in Japan, a number of organisations and publications protesting the harsher aspects of the occupation sprung up. Then, in 1931, the Japanese army invaded northern China, eventually reaching Shanghai in 1932. This new Sino–Japanese war was marked by atrocities on the part of the Japanese army, such as the 'rape of Nanjing', China's provisional capital at the time (1937–8). Chiang Kai-shek withdrew his government to Chungqing, where he would stay for the rest of the war.

'Big Brother' Wen-heung was right: the end of Japanese occupation didn't mean the end of Taiwan's sufferings. Momentarily united – after the Xi'an incident[12] – to defeat the Japanese invader, Mao Zedong's Communists and Chiang Kai-shek's Nationalists resumed the civil war in late 1945.[13] In spite of their initial superiority in number, the Kuomintang suffered a major defeat at the end of 1948. On 21 January, Chiang resigned as president but retained his position as head of the Kuomintang. Ten days later, PLA troops entered Beijing, then gained control over the rest of the country. The People's Republic of China (PRC) was proclaimed in Tiananmen Square on 1 October 1949. Kuomintang officials had long been ready for a possible defeat. Reclaiming Taiwan in 1945, Chiang had appointed Chen Yi – former governor of the Fujian province – governor of Taiwan, with the mission to repress any local opposition. As early as 1946–7, rich families and company executives packed their assets and started emigrating to Taiwan, followed by more modest people who were either following their employers or simply, like Hou Hsiao-hsien's father himself, exploring better job opportunities. At the beginning of Hou's autobiographical *The Time to Live and the Time to Die* (1985), a voice-over states:

In 1947, 39 days after my birth, my father took the local sports team to Guangzhou. There he met a friend, the mayor of Tai-cheung, Taiwan, who offered to become his deputy. A year later my father wrote to us that in Taiwan life was good and they had running water, so he invited us to come and join him.

Throughout 1948, Nationalist troops (as many as 300,000) were shipped to the island, along with 'war treasures' of historical art, and finally the Nationalist army crossed the Taiwan straits by boat. The number of this mass exodus is estimated at one and a half million (including 600,000 soldiers), bringing the Taiwanese population to 7 million. As soon as the mainlanders – who, for the most part, spoke Mandarin, which was to become the island's official language – had arrived in Taiwan, tension erupted between them and the 'native Taiwanese'.[14] Originally, the Kuomintang had intended to use Taiwan as a mere base to regroup before invading the mainland and taking it back from 'Communist bandits'. The island became forcibly enlisted in the anti-Communist struggle. Tension culminated in bloody confrontation on 28 February 1947 between mainlanders and Taiwanese, which was the beginning of the 'White Terror' imposed by the Kuomintang in the early 1950s – later the subject of Hou's *Good Men, Good Women* (1995). In 1948, Chen Yi (the main architect of the repression following the February incident) imposed martial law, which lasted till 1987. In 1949, the Kuomintang officially took control of the island.

National Identity and New Taiwanese Cinema

From then on – and roughly till the early 1990s – Taiwan was to live a strange brand of political fiction. The Nationalist Party asserted itself as the only legitimate source of power for the *entire* China, and representatives from various mainland provinces, elected before 1949 and becoming more and more ancient, were still sitting in the National Assembly. The subject of a 'Taiwan identity' was taboo until the late 1970s, and every allusion to 'Taiwanese independence' was punishable by prison terms. This was not without effect on the arts and literature.

Because of the Japanese occupation, Taiwan was not involved, as other Asian countries were, in the discovery of early cinema after 1895. In mainland China, the first spectacle of 'electric shadows' took place in 1896 in Shanghai. Cinema reached Taiwan in 1901, but, for all intents and purpose, the films produced on the island till 1937 (the date of the Sino–Japanese war that virtually interrupted all activity) represent a footnote in the history of Japanese cinema. However, during that time, cinema had become a popular form of entertainment, the most remote villages using a generator and a white cloth as a screen in order to put on open-air film shows accompanied by a *benshi*[15] – renamed *benzi* by the Taiwanese – as Wu Nien-jen (one of Hou Hsiao-hsien's screenwriters who eventually became a director) depicts in his autobiographical film, *A Borrowed Life* (1994).

In the early 1950s, Taiwanese cinema was represented by two types of production. Discouraged by the Nationalist Party, who had long sought to use cinema to impose Mandarin Chinese all over China, but much loved by the local population, there was a flurry of low-budget Taiwanese-language productions – the most informed studies[16] reckon that the number of such films made in Taiwan between the late 1940s and the early 1970s was between 1000 and 1500. On the other hand, the Kuomintang created well-funded studios, the most important being the Central Motion Picture Corporation (CMPC), which was to play a central role in the Taiwanese film industry. After 1955, Taiwanese-language films, with lesser production values, gradually declined, then stopped altogether. The first CMPC productions had been mediocre propaganda pieces, but the government efforts to endow Taiwan with a significant film industry, especially in collaboration with the more experienced Hong Kong producers, were paying off. Then, in 1971, Taiwan lost its seat in the United Nations at the expense of the PRC; in 1979 the United States broke with Taiwan and established diplomatic relations with the PRC. This was the beginning of a long period of diplomatic isolation that would stop only in 1996 with the first democratic elections and the threat of Chinese missiles over the Taiwan straits.

In the late 1970s, the film industry, having gradually retreated into escapist productions (kung-fu, romances, historical epics), was in a major crisis. Convinced that cinema could become an important diplomatic tool, the Kuomintang decided to 'revitalise' it. The 'New Taiwanese Cinema' was born out of these unlikely circumstances and it was, paradoxically, the official studio of the Kuomintang, the CMPC, which made it possible.

In 1980, the newly appointed director of the CMPC, Ming Ji, asked 28 year-old Wu Nien-jen to join the studio. A short story writer and novelist, Wu had just collaborated on his first screenplay. 'It was easier', remembers Wu, 'to promote change within the CMPC than in independent production companies, who knew nothing about the new generation of film directors. The CMPC belongs to the Kuomintang, it's very rich; they didn't care if you lost money, so you were actually free to try new things.'[17] At the end of 1980, another young writer, Hsiao-yeh, joined the CMPC and teamed up with Wu. The first project they initiated was *In Our Times* (1982), an omnibus film about changes in contemporary Taiwanese society, written and directed by four young directors: Edward Yang (who was to become, with Hou, the most important exponent of the New Taiwanese Cinema),[18] Chang Yi (another important *auteur* of the 'movement'), Tao Dechen and Ko Yi-cheng.

After the success of the film, Wu Nien-jen and Hsiao-yeh contacted two directors, Chen Kuen-hou and Hou Hsiao-hsien. The latter had

Portrait of Hou Hsiao-hsien

entered the film industry almost by accident. His semi-delinquent youth had, luckily, been cut short by military service.[19] Upon his discharge, he completed some perfunctory studies at an art school, did a series of odd jobs, then started in the film industry as a continuity person, graduating to assistant director and screenwriter, a double position he was to occupy for several years. In 1980, he wrote and directed his first feature, *Cute Girl*, a romantic musical comedy that was quite successful, followed by another work in the same vein, *Cheerful Wind* (1981). While his third feature, *Green, Green Grass of Home* (1982) follows roughly the same pattern (being a vehicle for the Hong Kong singer/actor Kenny Bee), it already marks a change, as Hou's screenplay is inspired not by a candy-coloured fantasy but by real stories told to him by his siblings, who were schoolteachers in rural areas.

In a literary magazine, Hou read a short story by a young female novelist, Chu Tien-wen, which impressed him a lot. 'We met in an old cafe in Taipei. We got along quite well, and I asked her to write a screenplay with me.'[20] The resulting film, *Growing Up* (1983), co-written by Chu and Hou, directed by Chen Kuen-hou and produced for the CMPC by Wu Nien-jen and Hsiao-yeh, is one of the founding works that paved the way for the achievements of the New Taiwanese Cinema. The same year, Wu Nien-jen wrote three screenplays inspired by the short stories of Hwang Chun-ming,[21] maybe the best-known exponent of a cultural and literary movement that emerged in the mid-1970s in Taiwan – *hsiang-t'u wen-hsueh*, or 'nativist literature': 'sympathetic stories about the … daily life of farmers, workers, prostitutes, small businessmen and so on. Much of the dialogue was written in Taiwanese dialect, with earthy profanities … In 1977, the authorities attacked this genre as "worker-peasant-soldier-literature", an allusion to the Communists' literary philosophy. This only fueled its popularity.'[22] Wu acknowledges his debt to this literary movement:

Before, most writers were influenced by European or American writers. After 1970, they turned their heads to Taiwanese subjects. [Under Hwang Chun-ming's influence], we came to believe that we had to pull the film industry into our own world, instead of imitating melodramas from the West.[23]

Then Wu produced another omnibus film, asking three young film-makers to each direct a half-hour episode based on his treatment of Hwang's stories. The episode directed by Hou, *His Son's Big Doll* (1983), gives its title to the whole film (in English *The Sandwich Man*); the two other stories, *Vicky's Hat* and *The Taste of Apples,* were entrusted to Tseng Chuang-hsiang and Wan Jen, respectively.[24] With *The Sandwich Man*, the New Taiwanese Cinema was officially born, and Hou Hsiao-hsien had completely changed his directing style – via the neo-realist approach of *His Son's Big Doll* he was striving to reclaim and illustrate the lives of real Taiwanese people struggling with social and economic change. The next step was an investigation of his own troubled youth, in *The Boys from Fengkuei* (1983), written by Chu Tien-wen. The film was produced by the CMPC, which, the same year, also produced *That Day on the Beach*, directed by Edward Yang from a screenplay he had co-written with Wu Nien-jen. From then on and till the moment he started directing his own films, Wu was to sign or contribute to an astonishing number of new Taiwanese films: in the mid-1980s, he was penning an average of four to five screenplays a year.

The early 1980s was the honeymoon period of the New Taiwanese Cinema and a time of enthusiasm, energy and excitement. A real solidarity and aesthetic kinship existed between the directors. In 1985, still under the auspices of the CMPC, Hou produced and starred in Yang's second feature, *Taipei Story*, whose screenplay was a collaboration between Yang, Hou and Chu Tien-wen. A year before, Yang had appeared in a small role – as the father of the two young protagonists – in Hou's *A Summer at Grandpa's* (1984) in which Chu Tien-wen recreated an episode of her own childhood. In his next film, *The Time to Live and the Time to Die*, Hou explored the history of his family, from their arrival in Taiwan when he was a small child to the death of his grandmother and his entry into the adult world. *Dust in the Wind* (1986) was the fond remembrance of a love affair experienced by Wu Nien-jen when he was a young man. This was followed by *Daughter of the Nile* (1987), the first of Hou's post-*Sandwich Man* films to take place in contemporary time. The film was described at the time as a radical change in his work, but Hou views it in a different light, as a step toward the making of *A City*:

In *A Summer at Grandpa's*, *The Time to Live*, and *Dust in the Wind*, Chu Tien-wen, Wu Nien-jen and I were using our personal experience. Then, we wanted to move away from this material, and that's what we did with *Daughter of the Nile*. And, in *A City of Sadness*, we got involved in something we had never dealt with before, but we used our understanding of human beings we had accumulated through our work. So it didn't matter whether or not we made a film taking place in modern times or in an era none of us had experienced. I don't think, anyhow, that *A City* is a realistic representation of what happened – it is my subjective view, my 'imitation' of that time, it remains an imaginary world.[25]

2 A Family in the Wind of History

After the birth of Wen-heung's son, the Lin family gathers around the patriarch, Lin Ah-lu (Li Tien-lu) to celebrate the opening of their new venture, a nightclub and gambling house called 'Little Shanghai'. The second and third sons, Wen-sung and Wen-leung, having been drafted into the Japanese army, are still missing. The same day, the young nurse Hinomi (Hsin Shu-fen) arrives to take her new position at Kinguichu Miners' Hospital; since her brother, Hinoe, is busy teaching, he has asked his friend, Wen-ching (Tony Leung), the fourth son of the Lin family, to meet her.

As the Japanese are leaving the island, Hinomi parts with her friend, Shisuko (Nakamura Ikuyo), and spends more and more time with Hinoe (Wu Yi-fang) and his intellectual and socialist friends. Wen-leung, the Lin family's third son (Jack Kao) finally comes back, seriously damaged and shellshocked. Once he has recovered, he hooks up with a group of unsavoury characters – the Taiwanese 'Red Monkey' (Ai Tsu-tu) and a group of Shanghai gangsters, who convince him to take part in a scheme involving his brother's shipping business.

Red Monkey introduces Ah-ga (Kenny Cheung), the brother of Wen-heung's concubine, to his 'woman', the bar hostess Ah-tsun, and attempts to involve him in the distribution of counterfeit Japanese money. Shortly thereafter, Red Monkey is killed and the money disappears. Ah-ga gets scolded by 'Big Brother' Wen-heung when the latter discovers that he, Wen-leung and their gangster friends from Shanghai have used his ships and storehouse to smuggle illegal goods. In a gambling house, Wen-leung recognises one of the hostesses as Ah-tsun, now under the 'protection' of one of the mainland gangsters, Kim-tsua. The gangsters beat Wen-leung up. In spite of an attempt at mediation organised by Wen-heung, the Shanghai gang use their mainland connections to denounce the Lin brothers as Japanese collaborators. While Wen-heung narrowly escapes, Wen-leung is arrested by Nationalist soldiers. Wen-heung and Ah-ga organise a meeting with the Shanghai gangsters, and eventually obtain his release. However, Wen-leung has been so hideously tortured in jail that he is now reduced to state of permanent infancy.

Meanwhile, Hinomi and Wen-ching have developed a special friendship, based on their exchange of written notes whose content appears as intertitles on the screen. Upon visiting the Lin family, Hinomi learns that, while Wen-sung, the second son, is still missing in the Philippines, his wife keeps waiting for him and cleans his medical instruments every day. She also becomes friends with Ah-shue (Huang Tsien-ru), one of 'Big Brother' Wen-heung's daughters and Wen-ching's favourite niece.

On the eve of the 28 February incident, Hinoe and Wen-ching go to Taipei. The Miners' Hospital becomes a shelter for the wounded, who arrive in the middle of the night. Governor Chen Yi speaks on the radio, announcing various measures, and finally the pronouncement of martial law. Wen-ching arrives at the hospital but faints. Later, through handwritten notes and a flashback sequence, he recounts being violently threatened by Taiwanese thugs who suspected him of being a mainlander, because of his deafness, until Hinoe intervened. Hinoe returns a few days later, with an injured foot, explaining that more killings and arrests are taking place in Taipei. Hinomi and Hinoe seek refuge in their parents' ancestral home, but their father slaps his son and orders him to find another hiding place. He also prevents Hinomi from leaving the house. From her correspondence with Ah-shue, she learns that Wen-ching has been arrested.

Kept in a small cell with other young men, Wen-ching understands, in his world of silence, that summary trials and executions are taking place around him in the jail. However, after being taken to court, he is released and returns, sad and depressed, to the Lin family house. Next, he goes to visit the widow of one of his cellmates who was executed, and then disappears on a mysterious trip. Upon his return, he finds Hinomi involved in domestic chores in the Lin family house. Via writing and flashbacks, he tells her that he found Hinoe, now married and living in the mountains with a guerrilla group. Later, 'Big Brother' Wen-heung, restless on account of having had to close the business after the events of February and March, scolds him for not proposing to Hinomi and then storms out of the house to go gambling with Ah-ga. In the restroom of the gambling house, Ah-ga recognises one of the gangsters responsible for Wen-leung's arrest and a fight ensues. Ah-ga is wounded and Wen-heung is shot dead. Shortly after Wen-heung's funeral, Hinomi and Wen-ching are married. Hinomi gives birth to a little boy, Ah-chien. One night, they receive the news that Hinoe and his comrades have been arrested and killed by the military. In a letter sent to Ah-shue, Hinomi writes that a few days later, Wen-ching was arrested again and that she has no news of him.

Hinoe and Wen-ching arguing in the guerrilla camp

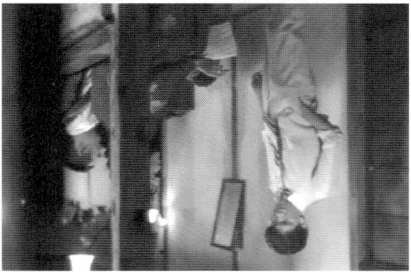

Wen-leung recognizes Ah-tsun, Red Monkey's former mistress

Photographic portrait of the Lin family

Of all the men of the Lin family, only the patriarch and the terminally damaged Wen-leung have survived.

The Actors

Since *The Boys from Fengkuei*, Hou had avoided using professional actors, dissatisfied by the kind of acting that was available in the Taiwanese film industry. His decision to work with non-professionals has had an impact on his aesthetics, prompting him to favour long takes and mundane actions over quick editing and melodramatic dialogues:

It is difficult for non-professionals to respond quickly in front of the camera, so the long takes provide them with a chance to develop their emotions slowly. I also design some daily life actions – such as washing clothes or eating – for them to perform, which gives them a chance to familiarize themselves with the situation.[26]

In *A City of Sadness*, most of the cast is composed of non-professionals: 'I wanted the extras to be the inhabitants of Giu Fen, because when they walk, they do it lightly, thinking of something else. People are like a landscape, they belong to one specific place.'[27] Located on the north coast of Taiwan, Giu Fen is a former gold mining town, where Hou had already shot *Dust in the Wind* and where most of the action of *A City* takes place.[28]

However, the production company, Era International, insisted on casting a famous Hong Kong star. The honeymoon between the 'New Taiwanese Cinema' and the CMPC was over and most directors were looking for other sources of financing. In 1981, Hou and three other film-makers had created their own production company, 'Ten Thousand Youths', later streamlined and renamed, first 'Marlboro' and then (in 1993) '3-H'. *Dust in the Wind* was the last film Hou shot in collaboration with the CMPC. For *Daughter of the Nile* he worked with a small independent company, Hsueh-Fu Films, that went bankrupt shortly afterwards. *A City* and *The Puppetmaster* (1993) were produced by Chiu Fu-sheng's company, Era International, which had started to get involved in film production in 1987 – and was also to produce Zhang Yimou's *Raise the Red Lantern* (1991), in which he involved Hou as an executive producer (as an 'advisor' to recreate the erotic decadence pervasive in the upper classes of Chinese feudal society). A well-travelled, well-educated businessman, Chiu Fu-sheng wanted to reach the international market. To seduce Japanese audiences, he contracted the services of the composer Naoki Tachikawa, famous at the time for having scored Juzo Itami's international box-office hits, *A Taxing Woman* (1987) and *The Return of a Taxing Woman* (1988). While Chiu prided himself on giving the maximum freedom to directors, he nevertheless suggested that one of the leads of *A City* should be Tony Leung Chiu-wai. A short, secretive actor who works more through his eyes than through his facial expression or body language, he was long mistaken by Western audiences for his almost-namesake, Tony Leung Ka-fai (after the latter starred in Jean-Jacques Annaud's *L'Amant* in 1992). His role in *A City* won him an international art house following, strengthened by his second collaboration with Hou in *Flowers of Shanghai* (1998).

In between the two films, Leung's career had blossomed, mostly due to his pivotal role in Wong Kar-wai's cinema – from a fleeting moment at the end of *Days of Being Wild* (1990) to major parts in *Chungking Express* (1993), *Ashes of Time* (1994), *Happy Together* (1997) and, finally, the Palme d'Or for Best Actor in *In the Mood for Love* (2000). He also worked twice with John Woo, in *A Bullet in the Head* (1990) and *Hard Boiled* (1992), and starred in Tran Anh Hung's *Cyclo* (1995). At the time of *A City*, Leung was well known to Hong Kong audiences for his work on television. He had also graced three *auteur* films. In *Love onto Waste* (1986), Stanley Kwan's second feature, Leung plays an apparently careless playboy who reveals, in the midst of a murder investigation, unsuspected psychological depth and a wounded soul. In Derek Yee's *People's Hero* (1987) – an artful remake of *A Dog Day's Afternoon* – he appears as a marginalised street punk who botches a robbery. In Patrick Tam's bloody and scintillating *My Heart is that Eternal Rose* (1988), he is an efficient yet ambiguous thug, with romantic longings and a secret death wish. Leung's uncanny capacity to project internal conflicts through minimal acting was well suited to

Tony Leung (left) in *Flowers of Shanghai*

Hou. Casting him as Wen-ching, the fourth brother of the Lin family, however, posed a major problem to the production.

With *A City*, Hou wanted not only to shoot his first sync sound film, but also to become an inspiration, a model and a provider of resources for the Taiwanese film industry. Hou and his sound engineer, Du Du-jih, had already experimented with sync sound in a few isolated cases, and conducted experiments in 16mm. For *A City*, they only had access to a Nagra reel-to-reel recorder, and two mono microphones. Later, encouraged by the success of the film, Hou gave Du Du-jih a large sum of money to acquire sync sound recording equipment that could be made available to other film-makers shooting in Taiwan as well.[29]

Until then, post-recording had been the norm in the three Chinas – due to the lack of good sound equipment, and also because it is easier, and faster, to shoot MOS (without sound). Until the early 1990s, in the Hong Kong and Taiwan film industries, which had been intertwined since the 1960s, dubbing made it possible to mix Taiwanese and Hong Kong actors in the same film. So, every film had two versions – one in Mandarin for the Taiwanese market, one in Cantonese for the Hong Kong and south-east Asian markets. Following this pattern, using Tony Leung would have meant dubbing him in Mandarin, which was unacceptable to Hou – even though he had to resort to doing so, years later, in the Japanese-financed *Flowers of Shanghai*.

According to Wu Nien-jen, 'The original … story was about a Hong Kong man coming to Taiwan to look for his uncle who had disappeared at the time of the Japanese surrender … Through his involvement with a

Taiwanese family, he would have learnt about the February 28 incident.'[30] Yet, as the project evolved, Hou and his screenwriters found a much more interesting solution – one that completely changes the structure of *A City*, turning the character of Lin Wen-ching into a metaphor for Taiwan's situation at that time: an observer of its own fate, without the right to speak for itself. As a deaf-mute, Wen-ching is one of the centres of gravity anchoring the fiction. His 'literary' exchanges with Hinomi constitute a metrical scansion within the film, 'emptying' the screen of visual content to replace it with a dark space, onto which white characters are printed – weaving another strand of the dialectic between the visible and the invisible on which *A City* is based (see Chapter Four). Incapable of hearing any sound, Wen-ching is nevertheless constantly surrounded by a dense tapestry of music, songs, voices, footsteps and more or less frightening noises. As he only became deaf after a childhood accident, *sound is for Wen-ching a memory* – a powerful idea and narrative device in a film predicated upon the retrieval of repressed collective memory.

In the first hour of the film, as Hinoe and his friends are discussing the current political situation – the food shortage, the corruption of Kuomintang officials and so on – Wen-ching *puts a record on*, with Hinomi looking at him. The music is an adaptation of a German folk song, and, in the intertitles that follow, Hinomi explains the legend of the Lorelei to him. Wen-ching replies to her:

> I could hear before I was eight.
> I remember the sound of goat bleating,
> the voice of the singer in the local opera.

The image cuts to a flashback – a makeshift opera stage in a courtyard, the singer performing, little boys watching and mimicking the operatic gestures – as the 'Lorelei' music gradually fades out under the high-pitched sound of Chinese opera. The sequence is one of the most beautiful and accurate representations of the genesis of love I know of in contemporary cinema – the sharing and communication of two mental universes (images, sensations, stories, dreams) between two human

First exchange of written notes between Hinomi and Wen-ching

Hinomi and Wen-ching 'listening' to the *Lorelei* record

The explanatory intertitle

'I fell from a tree when I was eight'

Opera performance in the courtyard

Little boys mimicking the performance

beings, and the slow impregnation of one by the other. Hinomi translates into writing spoken words that the deaf-mute no longer has access to, and he replies by invoking for her a world of past sensual memories.

Later, when Wen-ching is imprisoned in the aftermath of the 28 February incident, he shares a small cell with several other young men. Like Bresson's protagonist in *A Man Escaped* (1956), their only connection to the rest of the jail is through sound – the footsteps of guards coming and going, the creaking of the key turning in the door, the brief orders signifying the prisoners to 'appear in court', the defiant but melancholic singing of condemned men on their way to death, the brutal, definitive sound of gunshots. As members of the audience, we are privy to these sounds and can reconstruct what is happening only through them, as we are never given an establishing shot of the prison, nor an explanation of what is going on. We are in a situation similar to Wen-ching's cellmates – powerless witnesses of scenes of arbitrary violence. Yet, the man chosen to bear testimony of this ordeal is a deaf-mute, who experiences it *not through his ears but through his eyes*. While Wen-ching cannot hear the orders to 'go to court' nor the gunshots that result from summary 'trials', he *perceives* them through the body language of his cellmates. Hence the power of the shot in which we see Tony Leung's expressive face, behind bars, framed by the cell window, *reacting at the sound of two gunshots*.

It is no accident that, having made him a deaf-mute, Hou turned Wen-ching into a photographer, an intense witness of his time, capable of extracting emotions, narrative, spirituality, from framing and lighting his subjects. Having turned the 'necessity' of using a Hong Kong star into a major structuring device to his advantage, Hou had also crafted the part in his customary manner – by imitating life. Specific aspects of Wen-ching's personality and history were inspired by Hou's friendship with a painter,

Wen-ching retouching a photograph

Cheng Tinshi, who had become deaf after falling from a tree at the age of eight and communicated with people through written notes.[31]

On the other hand, the actress playing Hinomi, Hsin Shu-fen, had been part of Hou's 'family' since *The Time to Live and the Time to Die*. She was barely 18, and studying in a business college, when Hou met her in the Hsimen Din neighbourhood in the centre of Taipei, where young people like to hang out. Hou auditioned Hsin for *The Time to Live*, then offered her the part of one of the protagonist's sisters. In *Dust in the Wind*, she is a small-town girl, A Yun, who moves to Taipei with her boyfriend, A Yuan, in the hope of finding a job, and then marries another man during the long term of A Yuan's military service. In *Daughter of the Nile* she stars as Shiao-yang, a cop's teenage daughter who, after her mother's death and during

Hsin Shu-fen in *Daughter of the Nile*

her father's absences, assumes the responsibility for her family – she cooks, cleans, works as a waitress, and goes to night-school while pursuing a rich fantasy life (she identifies with the heroine of her favourite comic-book). In Hsin Shu-fen, Hou found what no 'professional' actress could have given him: the mixture of ordinariness and restrained passion that a 'normal' young Taiwanese woman could project. Pretty without being glamorous, she is quiet and thoughtful, attentive to her surroundings and to those around her – the quintessential Hou Hsiao-hsien character. She is aware that time will eventually rob her, like dust in the wind, of what she holds dearest. Instead of desperately throwing herself into the pleasures of the moment, like Annie Shizuka Inoh in *Good Men, Good Women* and *Goodbye South, Goodbye* (1996) or Shu Qi in *Millennium Mambo* (2001), she meditates on her feelings, her longing, her fulfilment. For Hsin, happiness is already a memory and, precisely for this reason, she will treasure it for ever. *A City* was to be her last film; shortly afterwards she married and moved to the United States.

Shu Qi (centre) in *Millennium Mambo*

At the other end of the spectrum, Chen Sown-yung ('Big Brother' Lin) *was* a known professional actor. While Taiwanese-speaking films had mostly disappeared, television continued to provide entertainment and drama in that language. Speaking and performing only in Taiwanese, Chen is the living representative of the popular, traditional aspects of Taiwan that stubbornly refuse to die. Usually cast 'in character' for his stout, powerful physique, his loud, throaty voice and his impressive body language, Chen also appeared – in gangster roles – in a few movies in the 1980s and early 1990s. A colourful personality, Chen candidly admitted to patronising prostitutes and dealing in precious gems and stones as a 'side-line'. A grass-roots character, he lived, at the time of *A City*, in a small working-class apartment with his brother's family and regaled visitors with lively conversations while ritualistically preparing tea, Taiwanese style. A brief example of his know-how in that domain appears in a sequence of *A City*. As the eldest son, Chen's character holds the Lin family together; he runs the business, scolds his siblings when they stray, negotiates with the

Young gangsters before the arbitration meeting

Big Brother Wen-heung waiting for the Shanghaiese gangsters

mainland gangsters. Yet, after the 28 February incident, this man who seemed strong as a rock starts to unravel. Hou shows him, in a quiet moment, sitting silently and mournfully in the house of Wen-ching, who has just been arrested. Later, forced to close his nightclub, he takes to drinking and gambling, quarrels with his wife, and yells at the folk musicians that his father has invited to perform in the house. However, just before leaving, in anger, for the gambling house where he will be fatally shot, he yells an ultimate piece of advice to the deaf Wen-ching, shaming him for not proposing to Hinomi. His daughter, Ah-shue, transcribes his speech for Wen-ching, who later carries this legacy, marrying Hinomi shortly after his brother's funeral.[32] Chen Sown-yung's presence anchors the fiction in a sort of existential realism. After his death, time seems to flow in a more surreal way – in a series of disjointed episodes that tread lightly throughout Hinomi's pregnancy, the birth of little Ah-chien, the news of Hinoe's death, and Wen-ching's off-screen arrest and disappearance.

Grandpa Lin at the wedding

Li Tien-lu in *Daughter of the Nile*

Li Tien-lu (Grandpa Lin) was also a well-known performer in Taiwan – where he was awarded a monthly pension as a 'National Treasure'. Born in 1910 during the Japanese occupation, Li was an accomplished puppetmaster, who had achieved international recognition and had travelled, performed and taught puppetry in France. The practitioner of a traditional folk art, he was a typical Taiwanese – in his language, his manners, his lifestyle – as well as a fascinating storyteller. After *A City*, Hou was to construct *The Puppetmaster* around his personality, by asking him to recount his memories in front of the camera, alternating them with fictional creations. Hou made four films with Li – each time casting him 'in type' as a garrulous, feisty, sincere, cantankerous, grand old man, with always the necessary touch of distancing irony. There was a hidden sensuality (a taste for good food, fine music and fine women), as well as an immense generosity and an impeccable sense of pacing in his small, wiry, energetic body. In *Dust in the Wind*, he welcomes his grandson, A Yuan, at the train station when he comes back from his military service and gently, humorously softens the blow of his girlfriend's desertion. As the grandfather of the heroine of *Daughter of the Nile*, his smiling presence lightens the screen. In *A City*, Hou gives him lines that indirectly allude to his own survival skills during the Japanese occupation: 'The Japanese government said I was a gangster. Me, a gangster? … I was only trying to help the district – make big problems into little ones, and little problems into no problems …' Li Tien-lu died in 1998 – his inimitable, rasping voice, his stories forever preserved in Hou's work.

As third brother Wen-leung, Jack Kao (aka Kao She-lin) has an opaque presence. At first, his whereabouts are unknown, then, when he reappears, prone to uncontrollable fits, he has to be immediately hospitalised. What happened to him during the war, in Shanghai, is only hinted at through hearsay, and his motivations, his personal history, as well as his private life (he is married with children, but we only see him interacting with his wife when he dementedly assaults her at the hospital) remain obscure. From his father, we learn that, even before going to war, he was already prone to 'trouble'. Uprooted, alienated from the traditional values still embodied by his father and older brother, seduced by the lifestyle of Shanghai gangsters, he is, for all his posturing, a confused, lost man. Finally, after being tortured in jail, he is reduced to being a non-character, a childish, idiotic man who cannot talk and gobbles the offerings put on the altar of the ancestors. So it was easy for Era International publicists to overlook his contribution: the programme notes prepared for the Venice Film Festival contain no biographical information about him. However, Jack Kao is essential to Hou's cinema – having appeared in *every film* the latter has directed since *Daughter of the Nile* (except *The Puppetmaster*). When Hou met him, he was a cook (see his dexterity in frying squid in the wok in *Goodbye South, Goodbye*) – and maybe a little bit of a gangster. In *Daughter of the Nile*, he is cast as the brother of the heroine, a young gangster-cum-gigolo who likes dark glasses and smart clothes, but is marked for death. Asserting a strong presence through his striking, stubborn, strangely handsome face and the intensity of his gaze, Kao projects an arresting mixture of macho cool

Jack Kao in *Goodbye, South, Goodbye*

and vulnerability – and often suffers a tragic fate. In *Good Men, Good Women*, he is shot in the arms of his lover. In *Goodbye South, Goodbye*, he wanders in search of an opportunity, or a solution, acutely conscious of being an anachronism, and his last journey is stopped short in an accident-wrecked car, from which we do not see him emerge. He sports a pigtail and long silk robes as the wealthy, somewhat cynical patron of one of the 'flowers of Shanghai', then displays his gangster tattoos in *Millennium Mambo*, a film in which, secretly smitten by the teenage charms of Shu Qi, he is disposed of by rival gangs, off-screen, in the frozen beauty of the Japanese winter.

Kao in *Daughter of the Nile*

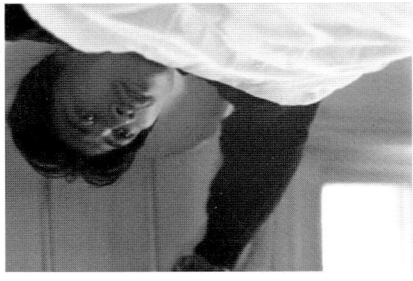

Wounded masculinity: Wen-leung tied to his hospital bed

The recurrence of the same performers throughout Hou's cinema, as well as the overlapping between their roles and their off-screen life, has the same effect as his repeated use of similar shots of the same real locations (see Chapter Four). On the one hand, it creates a stylised atmosphere, a vocabulary of forms and figures in which the spectator can eventually identify Hou's playful or tragic variations. On the other hand, a powerful 'effect of reality' is created, as the characters are speaking lines that may be fictional but resonate with their lives or their personal emotions or beliefs. The tension between fiction and documentary is particularly moving in *A City*, as, for the first time, we hear the actors' voices as they were uttered at the moment of the action. In the film, Taiwanese performers are asked to function as the living echoes of dramas that took place before their birth or when they were very small children (except for Mr Li Tien-lu, who had seen it all), but that had marked their parents and grandparents, and had been secretly passed to them. The past of the island vibrates through the bodies and voices of the actors in the present, *because they are themselves, as Taiwanese, shaped and produced by this history.* Which is why it makes sense that the only mute character should be played by a Hong Kong actor.

The Genesis of the Plot and the Controversy over the 28 February Incident

When Hou and his two screenwriters, Chu Tien-wen and Wu Nien-jen, set out to write *A City of Sadness*, they were conscious of the difficulties they would face in attempting to recreate a period of time they had not experienced and knew very little about. Born in a displaced family of mainlanders, Hou was at a further disadvantage, since in his childhood, contrary to Chu and Wu, he had not heard furtive conversations alluding to the 'events' of 1945–9. Before starting to work on *A City*, he 'only had a fragmentary knowledge of Taiwanese history'.[33] Yet he was lucky. In 1987, martial law was lifted and historical research became possible. Gradually, the taboo imposed upon the history of Taiwan began to disappear. *A City* would strike a fatal blow against it – leading the way for other major cinematic works re-examining Taiwanese history, as Wu Nien-jen explained:

People of my generation believe that if Taiwan has reached its current state, the reason lies in something that is buried in our history – forgotten because it was forbidden to discuss it. If Taiwan has become such a rich country, yet without culture and a sense of law, it's because for decades you couldn't talk openly about social and political issues. We have been taught that it's all right to become rich, but wrong to get involved in politics[34]

Banned from the public sphere, the recounting of Taiwanese history became confined to private conversations – at people's homes around a cup of coffee, in karaoke bars, teahouses or restaurants. The political became private, confidential, obscure, minute, intimate. Against the official history, uttered by the organs of the Kuomintang and divorced from the Taiwanese experience, a history of silence slowly emerged, halting the flow of images and sounds imposed from above to listen instead to these muted, anonymous voices talking in the darkness – creating what I called, in an earlier essay, a 'whispering cinema'.[35]

Thus, it is an intimate part of Hou's aesthetics that, since *A Summer at Grandpa's*, the process of screenwriting takes the form of *long, extended conversations*. *A City* represents the apex of the unique collaboration that united, for a brief period of time, Chu Tien-wen, Wu Nien-jen and Hou Hsiao-hsien. The setting was a traditional teahouse in the centre of Taipei. As demonstrated by Chen Sown-yung's sense of ritual or proven, later, in a conversation between gangsters at the beginning of *Goodbye South, Goodbye*, tea is a serious matter in Taiwan. It is an example of spontaneous, yet invisible, resistance to official history. The Nationalist Party wanted to eradicate the sense of Taiwanese *difference* and present the history of the island as a continuation of the history of mainland China. However, not even in Fujian does one find teas that taste like the ones picked on the highest mountains of Taiwan. Their purity, their fragrance, the subtle variety of their flavour is unique. The Taiwanese have a particular way of preparing and drinking tea. So, in this exquisitely decorated teahouse, a modest but potent signifier of indigenous culture, Hou and his two screenwriters would sit and talk for hours, gathering, discussing, discarding and structuring ideas. Sometimes friends would drop by, tea would be offered, remarks exchanged – and the whole organic, convivial process would feed the scenario.[36]

Since *The Boys from Fengkuei*, Chu Tien-wen has been Hou's main collaborator. While her father, a writer, came from mainland China after 1949, her mother belongs to an old Taiwanese Hakka family – which gave Chu, born in 1956, a sense of being 'rooted' in the island. She also grew up in a literary milieu. Hou, coming from an impoverished, displaced family, and without much formal schooling, was able to benefit from her innate sense of Taiwanese identity, as well as from her sophisticated pan-Chinese culture. As he was preparing *The Boys from Fengkuei*, Chu gave him the autobiography of the mainland writer Shen Congwen.[37] What Hou retained from the book was its 'panoramic view of events'[38] that inspired him to put the camera at a distance from the action represented.

A published writer since her late teens and an award-winning novelist, Chu had never written a screenplay before *Growing Up*. 'It was very long, with a lot of descriptions. This intrigued me a lot, because it conveyed a novelist's sense of atmosphere – and I decided to adopt this new way of thinking,' recalls Hou.[39] Chu Tien-wen defines her role as an 'echo', or a sounding board for Hou's ideas – listening to him, and then free-associating, interjecting comments, personal memories, feelings, 'sometimes without any direct connection to the screenplay'.[40]

When I write a screenplay I enter a realm where I do not belong – that of the image. My role consists in fixating the movement of Hou Hsiao-hsien's immense creativity in language. Creation puts you in a state of daydream. I try to accompany Hou in his dreams … I express things through words, and he through a pictural form of art.[41]

Both Hou and Chu agree that she helped him better define and understand his female characters. Femininity occupies a paradoxical place in Hou's universe. On the one hand, he has the nostalgia of a macho world of tough gangsters and petty thugs, the playfulness, roughness, and even 'primitivism' of competitive masculinity[42] – and this often influences his choice of collaborators (Chen Sow-yung, Jack Kao; a couple of associate producers in *A City* were karaoke club owners or former smugglers). On the other hand, as shown in *The Time to Live*, he grew up in a family of women, with a stoically silent, remote and sick father who died when he was young. Contrary to Edward Yang or to Wu Nien-jen, who see in the relationship between father and son one of the backbones of Chinese culture,[43] Hou structures his families around the presence of women. The paradox is that Hou's female characters

correspond to the three women he's known the most in his youth: his mother, older sister and grandmother. They are rather withdrawn, reserved, very patient, and capable of bearing a lot – they correspond to the traditional image of the Asian woman … For a long time, Hou didn't have the slightest idea of their inner lives …[44]

Indeed, the women portrayed in *A City* correspond to this description: the wives (and mistress) of the first three brothers of the Lin family are mere background characters and Hinomi is, from the outset, presented in relation to the three important men in her life – her father, her brother and Wen-ching. She is a reserved, patient woman, capable of bearing a lot – yet she is hardly silent. Her *voice* is one of the two main devices that carries the narration throughout (see Chapter Three). Moreover, she acts on her desire, as 'Big Brother' Wen-heung notes, both admiringly and angrily: 'For a girl to come to our house, with no regard for her self-respect … it's very clear what's going on!'

So, like the sexual politics in Hou's films, his collaboration with Chu Tien-wen weaves a complex network of reciprocal influences, exchange and 'translation' from one world to another. A feminist analysis might interpret – along lines suggested by Chu herself – woman on the side of the voice and man on the side of the image. However, it could also be deciphered in the light of Chinese cosmogony, as a dynamic interplay between *yin* and *yang* – considering they don't exist one without the other but complement each other: the essence of being is the movement that connects one to the other. In Hou's aesthetics, light is born out of darkness and silence out of noise – and also, because of the limpid, sensuous space–time continuum he creates, *light out of silence as well as darkness out of noise*. Similarly, *yin* denotes as well darkness, silence, cold, interiority and femininity; *yang* light, noise, warmth, exteriority and masculinity – among other multiple sets of dynamic oppositions on which the Chinese vision of the world is based.[45.] More essentially, the *yin* is the truth of the *yang* and vice versa. Chu Tien-wen does more than 'supply' words to channel Hou Hsiao-hsien's 'instinctual' and 'dreamlike' vision. She is *the other side, the ubac* of this vision; the interiority of the world of opaque and glittering surfaces his films are creating; the femininity hidden in him.

Hou's collaboration with Wu Nien-jen was short-lived but crucial. Wu was born in 1952, in rural Taiwan, in a family that had emigrated to the island more than 300 years before. At home they spoke Taiwanese, but his father, a miner, had been deeply marked by the Japanese occupation. Wu studied accounting at night while working during the day. To supplement his income, he would occasionally publish stories in newspapers, which started his career as a writer. Wu 'gave' the story of his youth to Hou Hsiao-hsien and Chu Tien-wen, who structured it into what was to become *Dust in the Wind*. *A City of Sadness* was his third collaboration with Hou (considering he had written the screenplay of *The Sandwich Man*), and in *The Puppetmaster*, his fourth and final one, he helped gather and structure Li Tien-lu's memories.

In 1994, Wu directed his first feature, *A Borrowed Life*, followed by *Buddha Bless America* in 1996. A well-known figure of the Taiwanese film world, Wu has also been cast in supporting roles, most notably as a hick gangster in Edward Yang's *Mahjong* (1996), before appearing as the main protagonist in Yang's *A One and a Two* (aka *Yi Yi*, 2000). In *A City*, he appears in a small cameo.

Wu is a more 'traditional' screenwriter than Chu – however, during the time of their collaboration, he gracefully lent himself to the idiosyncrasies of a more 'atmospheric', free-associating kind of writing that was endlessly modified as the work went along, and finally produced nothing but a blueprint designed to change again to fit the actors' speech mannerisms and body language.[46] In general, Wu's contribution was limited to writing the dialogue once Hou and Chu had designed the overall structure, but in *A City* his input started at the level of the huge gathering of information, anecdotes and stories that constitute the rich soil from which the film grows.

Parts of *A City* are inspired by stories that Wu heard in his home town while growing up.[47] Some were comical, such as the newly 'liberated' Taiwanese people not knowing which side of the Chinese flag the sun should be (is it rising from the bottom or setting at the top?). Some were tragic, as with the trip taken by the former cellmate of an executed man to bring his widow a letter written in blood on a piece of fabric. At the research stage, Hou, Chu and Wu cast a very large net. They read a great number of documents – historical accounts, novels and personal diaries – pertaining to the Japanese occupation and the 28 February incident. They conducted hundreds of interviews. A photographer commented on the pictures he had taken in the late 1940s. Later he introduced them to a man who had been a district magistrate during the Japanese occupation and turned out to be a mine of anecdotes. The photographer's great uncle was a boatman in the 1940s, and contributed stories about smuggling. Li Tien-lu, the puppetmaster, had many memories of that time – such as seeing corpses floating in a river. Other anecdotes came from the father-in-law of one of the producers and the father of the cinematographer, Chen Hwai-en. 'One of the executive producers was a smuggler at that time,' adds Hou, 'and contributed many stories. He's about 60 years old, and I gave him the small role of the man teaching the hospital staff how to speak Mandarin …'[48]

In digging into Taiwan's 'hidden history' of the late 1940s, Hou was taking risks. *The Time to Live* had already been attacked as a 'representation of the deceitful aspects of the official slogans about "taking back the mainland"'.[49] After completion of *A City*, the Nationalist government required two cuts. Yet, 'the press counter-attacked, and they backed down. The situation had changed, I was known abroad, they couldn't do anything against me.'[50] However, everything that had to do with the 28 February incident was still, in 1989, a highly sensitive and almost 'classified' matter – and in some parts of the country, the cuts were maintained.

The February incident – or 'Two-two-eight' as it is customarily referred to in Taiwan – occupies only a small portion of *A City* (no more than half an hour of screen time) and the violence is alluded to indirectly. Most Western critics, even when they describe the plot of the film in its political and historical context, fail to mention the incident. On the other hand, because 'to many [it] is *the* symbol of the Kuomintang's "foreign domination" over Taiwan's "native people"',[51] it is almost always at the centre of every text written by Chinese authors on the film. On 27 February, an elderly lady selling smuggled cigarettes in the street was brutally beaten by government agents; angered bystanders reacted, and in the ensuing scuffle, a man was killed. The next morning about 2,000 unarmed Taiwanese gathered in protest. They were met with machine guns. Riots erupted throughout the country, violent incidents took place between Taiwanese and mainlanders. Governor Chen Yi orchestrated a bloody repression whose death toll is estimated at several tens of thousands – crushing the demands for political reform, arresting

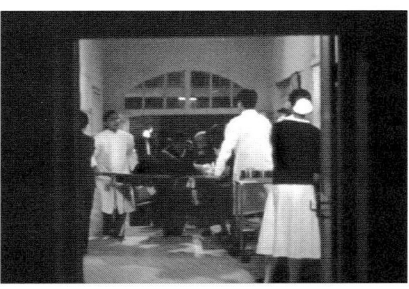

The wounded being brought to the hospital

Taiwanese nationalists attack Wen-ching

intellectuals and political leaders and paving the way for the White Terror
of the 1950s.

A City of Sadness had a tremendous, long-lasting effect on Taiwanese
audiences. In one of his earlier made-for-TV dramas, Four Corners of the
World (1989), Tsai Ming-liang shows spectators lining up in front of the
theatre to make sure they would get in, and poor people stockpiling tickets
to sell them at higher prices. However indirectly, 'Two-two-eight' was
finally *represented* – the mere *mention* of the incident had been forbidden
for over 40 years! 'When we were doing research on the film,' says Hou, 'I
realise that in Taiwanese families, nobody had dared to speak … When the
film came out, speech was liberated. It was like a huge wave breaking. An
internal block came undone all at once.'[52] Three years later, in 1992, the
government released the 'lengthy Executive Yuan task force report …
admitting that its army killed an estimated 18,000 to 28,000 native-born
Taiwanese in the 1947 massacre'.[53]

Big Brother Wen-heung before his son's birth

The first visual motif shot: a misty landscape at night.

Hinomi arriving at the hospital on a sedan

First instance of the visual motif shot of the hospital

Hinoe looking in Shisuko's direction

Shisuko at the piano in the classroom

Silence between Hinomi and Shisuko
after the exchange of gifts

Shisuko standing in the hospital
entrance

Shisuko in the red kimono

Shisuko's brother calligraphing a poem, while Hinoe is looking

Hinoe, Wen-ching and Hinomi looking at the poem

Wen-ching reading the story of the young Japanese woman

Wen-ching and his guide arrive at
Hinoe's guerrilla camp

The deaf man's glance: execution
shots on the soundtrack

Big Brother Wen-heung in Wen-ching's
empty house

Ah-kio's arbitration

Landscape in the mist with flying bird

Wen-heung's funeral

Hinomi and Wen-ching's wedding

Hinomi writing her diary on the kitchen table

A knock on the door

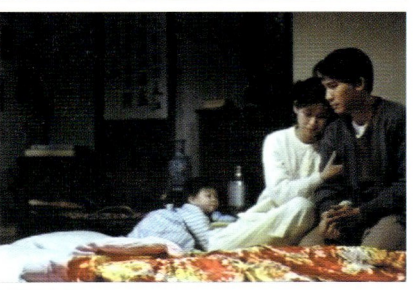

Hinomi and Wen-ching embrace

Calm landscape as the guerrillas are rounded up

The arrest of the guerrillas

Landscape: mountain, water, tree, wooden fence

On the platform

Preparing for the family portrait

The family portrait

The famous last shot of the empty
dining room

Dinner

Gambling in the Lin family dining room

Ah-shue reading Hinomi's letter

3 A Polyphony of Voices

The first sync sound film shot in Taiwan, *A City of Sadness* is also one in which the soundtrack is the most elaborate. The viewer is bathed in a sensuous symphony of ambient sounds – music, voices and silence, which glide over and merge within each other. This feeling of fluidity is produced by the sound editing strategy. The end of a sequence is often announced, a few seconds from the end of its last shot, by the sound of the sequence that is to follow – thus bridging expanses of time and space. For example, in the sequence mentioned in Chapter One when the mainland gangsters arrive at the hospital to visit third brother Wen-leung, the sound of a conversation that takes place later in Red Monkey's establishment is heard over the image of the hospital entrance: 'Business is the business of men, isn't it?' Often this device is used to introduce a flashback, paradoxically providing a soundtrack to the silent memories of the deaf-mute Wen-ching, thus connecting the present time (Wen-ching communicating with Hinomi) and the past (what he has experienced). This involves a contradiction *per se*: as in the prison sequence in which Wen-ching reacts to sounds *he cannot hear*, the content of his narrative flashback involves dialogue, ambient noises and so on. A particularly subtle instance of this takes place in the last third of the film, when Wen-ching returns from a mysterious trip. The sequence starts with a medium long shot of Hinomi, sitting at a kitchen table in the Lin family house, snipping string-beans and looking distraught. Behind her, a glass partition opens a vista to another room, where the altar to the ancestors stands. This shot, broken by a 15-second intertitle, lasts three and a half minutes – and then recurs, from exactly the same angle though for a shorter time, after the flashback sequence.

Off-screen, we hear the voice of Ah-shue, Big Brother Wen-heung's older daughter: 'Auntie Hinomi, Uncle's back!' The entire Lin family is taking for granted that Hinomi's frequent visits are due to her emotional involvement with Wen-ching – yet the two protagonists of this protracted courtship fail to acknowledge 'what is going on', and, as in the case of Shisuko and Hinoe, use their mutual concern for a sibling to express their feelings. Ah-shue enters from the right, followed by Wen-ching, who is carrying an elegant leather shoulderbag and looks a bit dazed. Hinomi stands up, but he motions her to sit down by slightly touching her arm. Ah-shue, who had disappeared on the right, reappears again and, as Wen-ching sits down, she takes his bag, exits a second time, then re-enters smiling, behind her uncle who is now sitting down at the table with Hinomi. An off-screen voice (obviously Ah-shue's mother) is heard, acknowledged by Ah-shue who leaves again, only to return a few seconds later with some writing material that she deposits on the table between the two young people, telling them, in a complicit tone: 'have fun writing'. She goes behind the glass partition and scolds Wen-leung for eating the altar offerings. A dim, out-of-focus presence, Wen-leung's body position and white shirt create an exact, shadowy parallel to the image of Wen-ching in the front, and the inarticulate sounds he produces in response to Ah-shue's scolding are an echo of those uttered by Wen-ching when he is upset – as we are *about to hear* in the flashback. As Ah-shue continues to talk to her Third Uncle in the background, and a series of footsteps are heard off-screen throughout the house, Wen-ching and Hinomi exchange written notes, and a first title appears: 'You're thinner. How's your health? Brother has disappeared …' After the title, the same silent exchange of notes resumes for about 45 seconds – during which one becomes aware that the *quality of the sound* has slightly changed, as if objects and off-screen footsteps were no longer resonating in the enclosed space of a house. A cut takes us into the long shot of a country road, in which a mobile camera follows two men walking – one of them being Wen-ching, carrying his shoulderbag, and their footsteps on the uneven ground are heard. The sound mix here involves the *sound reverberation* particular to two distinct spaces, indoor and outdoor.

What is remarkable about this flashback is that, while it is apparently the translation into images and sound of a narration made by Wen-ching of his visit to Hinoe's guerrilla camp in the mountains, it contains a conversation that the young man obviously *did not report to Hinomi*. When Wen-ching expresses his intention to join the guerrilla group, Hinoe refuses him – causing a violent reaction on the part of Wen-ching, whose entire body is shaken by frustration and anger, and who, in his distress, tries to speak. In writing, Hinoe uses a definitive argument: 'As to Hinomi, the family has received a [marriage] proposal. But I know that in her heart she is waiting for you … ' At the end of the flashback, we return to Hinomi at the kitchen table, half-crying, not as a young woman who has just heard that her brother is aware of her secret love and that the man she wants came back *for her*, but as one who realises in anguish that she will probably never see her brother again.

Hou inserts sound mixes of different levels of complexity throughout the film. The merging of two different musical sources occurs in the 'Lorelei' sequence discussed in Chapter Two. Another variation of this figure occurs when the sound of the next sequence 'spills over' the previous one to announce that the content of a letter is going to be disclosed – as in the sequence recounting Hinoe's arrest (see Chapter Five). This editorial strategy may be described as a form of *intellectual montage* applied to sound, as a sound is 'attracted' to a specific place within the structure of the film for reasons having to do with the content of the narration.

Another figure (almost the reverse of the one just discussed) is when diegetic sound is extended beyond the moment it is produced, so as to colour the entire sequence with a certain emotional tone. There is a fine example of this strategy in the 'Japanese flashback' that starts with the shot in which Hinoe looks at Shisuko sitting at the piano. She sings and plays *Aka Tonbo* ('Red Dragonfly'), a traditional children's song, taught in every Japanese school. Its lyrics have, like the poem written by Shisuko's brother, a double meaning. At a first level, they celebrate the beauty of nature in the autumn, with spectacular sunsets and many dragonflies about. On another, it is the story of a poor girl who takes a position as a babysitter in a rich family, but leaves them to contract an arranged marriage at 15, 'and then the letters home died out …'[54] So the song connotes the innocence of childhood marvelling at nature, but also melancholia: the narrator misses his young nanny, taken away by the unfairness of fate – a parallel to the aborted romance between Hinoe and Shisuko.

So even though, diegetically, the music no longer makes sense, it accompanies the entire sequence showing the warm and quiet friendship shared by Hinoe and the two Japanese siblings, as well as the moment – later in time – when Hinomi brings home the scroll on which Shisuko's brother had written his poem. Hinoe praises the love that the Japanese have for cherry blossoms, as ephemeral as life itself, and, as Wen-ching picks up the poem from the desk, the music stops so that the only sound is the ruffling of the elegant rice-paper.

From the beginning (Hirohito's speech) to the end (Tachikawa's music), *A City* is permeated through and through by Japanese sounds. Not only is the moody, emotional theme music heard at key moments, creating an aural scansion that contributed to the aesthetic success of the film, but a

The 'business meeting' between Wen-leung and the Shanghaiese gangsters

number of diegetic songs, in addition to *Aka Tonbo*, are Japanese. When Wen-ching is in jail, in a distant background, unseen prisoners break into a Japanese song, mourning the fate of young men going to war. That, at the moment of dying, victims of the Kuomintang repression turn to Japanese culture to express their feelings, is no accident. Like all film-makers forced by censorship to use subtle forms of expression, Hou resorts to discreet, apparently 'non-political' elements to make a point. The 'official history' the Nationalist Party sought to carve, in blood if necessary, onto the 'recovered' island was that Taiwan was an integral part of mainland China: the rupture in historical continuity created by 50 years of Japanese occupation had to be denied. Consequently, Japanese language and culture became the *signifiers of the specificity of the Taiwanese experience*. Which Kuomintang official could guess, by listening to an apparently innocuous nursery rhyme, that its hidden meaning was 'We are Taiwanese, *not* mainlanders'?

Taiwanese from all walks of life were deeply marked by Japanese culture. The 'Taiwanese dialect' itself, as it is spoken by the 'native' characters in the film, is laced with Japanese words and phrases. Moreover, among intellectuals and politically active people – like the ones most likely to be in the same jail as Wen-ching – turning back to Japanese culture meant taking a certain stance in relation to their own agency. As expressed many times in the film, by Hinoe's bookish friends as well as by the grass-roots 'Big Brother' Wen-heung, Taiwan kept being 'handed over' without being consulted, first by the Qing Dynasty to the Japanese and then by the Allies to the Nationalist Party.[55] Kept in a state of submission by the Japanese, the Taiwanese had hopes of becoming full citizens once they were reunited with the motherland. Instead, mainlanders were behaving in Taiwan as if in occupied territory. Reverting to Japanese mores and culture, to the language of the previous occupying forces, now defeated, was an understated way of *making a choice*, of rejecting the *present occupation*, of defiantly asserting that the gap between Taiwan and the mainland was unbridgeable.

The soundtrack of the first scene of *A City* – the birth of Wen-heung's son by his mistress, is an interesting synecdoche. As the cries of the expectant mother become louder and louder, Hirohito's voice starts fading out, until it is finally replaced by the drone of the theme music. Considering how 'hip' and commercially successful Tachikawa was at the time, the voice of traditional Japan – feudal, anachronistic, defeated – yields to the sounds of the economic giant on which Taiwan has tried to pattern its own modernity. This moment synthesises the entire arc-like movement of the film – from Hirohito's voice to Tachikawa's composition, which recurs in the last shot, over the image of the dining room, emptied by the destruction of the Lin family. The only thing left was Taiwan's entry into a capitalist economy – the 'Taiwan economic miracle' of the 1960s and 1970s – a process in which a growing interaction with Japan played a significant role. *A City of Sadness*, by its mode of production, was part and parcel of the new, thriving Taiwan, as Era International had contracted a pre-sales agreement with Japanese distributors. Even Hou's career, started in partnership with the CMPC, was forced into collaboration with Japanese and international capitalism: *Good Men, Good Women*, *Goodbye South, Goodbye* and *Flowers of Shanghai* were Japanese productions, and *Millennium Mambo* was financed by a French company. So, the final notes of Tachikawa's theme sound like a premonition.

In addition to Japanese, four languages are spoken throughout the film: Taiwanese, Shanghaiese, Cantonese and Mandarin. The members of the Lin family speak Taiwanese, with a few Japanese words interjected – as do Hinoe and Wen-ching's intellectual friends, except for a sympathetic mainland journalist, who expresses himself in Mandarin. Third Brother Wen-leung, who has learnt Shanghaiese during the war, switches back and forth between this dialect and Taiwanese. Big Brother's mistress and her brother Ah-ga come from Guangdong province, so they speak Cantonese, also mixed with Taiwanese.

The mainland gangsters with whom Wen-leung and Ah-ga tragically associate speak Shanghaiese, which creates a most interesting linguistic situation, when Big Brother Wen-heung and Ah-ga try to secure Wen-leung's release from the Kuomintang jails by negotiating with the gangsters who denounced him. Wen-heung's Taiwanese speech is translated into Cantonese by Ah-ga; one of the gangsters translates it in turn into Shanghaiese for the 'Big Bosses', and the conversation thus goes back and forth, with the translator sometimes inserting his own comments. In the international version, the subtitlers opted to paraphrase the different lines of dialogue. Wen-heung says: 'Our Wen-leung is in prison. I know you're well connected with officials. I would like to ask for your help. See if Wen-leung can be freed before the new year.' Ah-ga speaks in Cantonese: 'Wen-leung has been arrested. You know people in the right places. What Big Brother means is, we'd like to see him freed before the new year.' Finally, the Shanghaiese translation (done by a gangster sporting dark sunglasses) says: 'They are talking about Wen-leung's case. They hope he can be freed before the new year.' Nonchalantly, the Shanghai boss, always seen wearing black silk robes, replies: 'When was Wen-leung arrested? I didn't know.' The bilingual gangster translates into Cantonese: 'They didn't

Multi-lingual negotiation table for the release of Wen-leung

Hinomi and Wen-ching in the Lin family house

know Wen-leung was arrested. What can we do to help?' This prompts a violent outburst (in Cantonese) on the part of Ah-ga: 'Don't fuck with me! I know you're behind it!' In turn, Wen-leung scolds him (in Taiwanese): 'Stupid idiot! Why are you telling them this?'

While being a homage to the rich cultural patchwork that characterises the island, this situation also expresses a tragic aspect of the Chinese condition – the wound of fractured identity, the sadness of not being able to understand other Chinese. In the diegesis, it functions as a misunderstanding and a masquerade of which the Lin family is the victim. Wen-leung *is* eventually released for the new year (as evidenced by a shot of a lion dance immediately following his return home), but he is permanently damaged.

The interplay of voices modulating, sometimes in turn, sometimes contrapuntally, their different range of sounds creates an almost operatic tone, while the subtle and rigid etiquette that presides over the negotiation turns it into a ritual. There are quite a few such 'negotiation scenes' in Hou's films – the most important taking place towards the end of *Goodbye South, Goodbye* and involving two rival sets of gangsters and politicians and a local official. Except in the case of the discussion pertaining to the release of a 'flower girl' from her madam in *Flowers of Shanghai*, most of these negotiations are 'the business of men' and exclude women except as 'hostesses'. Even in the original discussion in Red Monkey's club between the mainland gangsters and Wen-leung (another interesting moment when, at some crucial turning points of the conversation, mainlanders and Taiwanese either fail to understand each other or utter unflattering asides about the other party), the Shanghai boss rudely objects to the presence of female entertainers.

However, earlier in the film, following the assassination of Red Monkey over the 'counterfeit' money, Hou stages an arbitration scene in which the mediator is an elderly lady, Ah-kio. Wearing a bright red top that contrasts with the dark suits worn by the men, she greets them by stating the role she expects to play: 'I am honored that you have come to see me … It's said that even the sky, when torn, can be mended.' She is alluding to one of the most famous Chinese myths, which celebrates the rise and fall of an archaic female power: the story of the original Goddess Nü Wa, who mended the sky after it had been destroyed by war among the humans she had created out of clay.[56] When the discussion threatens to turn sour, she interrupts it, first by pouring tea, then by offering a sensible solution to split the money. The lady seems to hold a position of moral authority over the feuding gangsters who kowtow to her and bow to her superior wisdom. Again, while setting clear oppositions between the world (and the business) of men and that of women, between male action and female voice, Hou never falls into a schematic pattern, instead depicting a sexual order that is much more intricate and complex than it first appears. The age of the lady arbitrator is, obviously, an issue – young women are objects of desire and/or obedient daughters and wives, while, after a certain age, a woman receives all the respect due to a matriarch. By giving the lady arbitrator a diegetic voice, Hou creates a channel, albeit marginal in the fiction, for female agency, in sharp contrast with male impotence eventually signified by the off-screen death of the deaf-mute son.

A Film Carried by the Voices of Two Women

From the outset, Hou orchestrates the different layers of the narration
through two different instances of voice-over: a male voice (first Hirohito,
then Governor Chen Yi), representative of an unseen authority imposed
from the outside, and two female voices (Hinomi reading her diary and Ah-
shue exchanging letters with Hinomi) that, by contrast, come from *within*
the diegesis. Both are instances, albeit radically opposed ones, of what
Michel Chion calls an *acousmêtre* – a voice-over, often endowed with
authority, whose source is invisible.[57] In the case of Hirohito's voice, the
radio that transmits it is hidden within the house of Wen-heung's mistress.
While Chion states that every voice speaking on the radio is *acousmatic*, it
could be argued, however, that when a radio voice is used in cinema, the

Hinomi writing her diary

absence or presence of the receiver in the image endows this voice with a
greater or lesser omnipotence and ubiquity. In the case of Hirohito, it
matters little whether or not there is an actual radio in the room – his
message carries huge consequences for the entire island, and everybody can
hear it, or hear about it. Radio voices are often used in Hou's cinema as a
medium to carry authoritarian or official messages and to create a tension
between the disembodied, mechanical quality of their source and –
conversely – the domestic settings in which they are heard, the living bodies
receiving them and whose steps, mundane gestures, breathing, moaning and
small talk can be heard in counterpoint. In a significant scene in *The Time to
Live*, the women in A Ha's family – his sister, mother and grandmother – are
doing domestic chores, while the radio talks about the heroic duty of the

Taiwanese army to recover the mainland. The women talk and gossip among themselves *without alluding to or commenting on the broadcast* – reducing it to an insignificant background noise.

In *A City*, the use of radio voices creates another contrast – between the *language* of the broadcast and that of the listeners. The radio speaks in a *foreign* tongue, clearly imposed onto Taiwanese reality – giving a poignant meaning to the concept of *voice-over*. As noted before, Hirohito expresses himself in a rarefied, classical form of Japanese only used by the ruling class – and certainly not by his Taiwanese subjects. In the second instance when the radio plays a significant narrative role – the broadcasting of 'security measures' following the 28 February incident – Governor Chen Yi speaks a Shanghaiese-accented Mandarin, marking him as a hated mainlander, an invader. Hou unfolds a compilation of Chen Yi's speeches, as the situation evolves. The first one starts over a deserted shot of mountains overlooking the sea, during the day, which has the same framing and the same angle as the night landscape shot following the 'birth sequence' at the beginning of the film – what I call a 'visual motif shot' (see Chapter Four). 'Compatriots of Taiwan, on the evening of the 27th, in Taipei, someone was unfortunately killed during an investigation ...' The speech is mixed with the droning tones and percussion music of the theme. It is carried over the next shot – in which nurses and doctors are listening to the radio receiver in the hospital office, looking worried: 'As for those who killed ... I have sent them to court to be tried severely ...'

There is a cut to a 'visual motif shot' of the hospital hallway, as Chen Yi's voice continues, announcing he's arranged for 'proper compensation'

Radio as *acousmètre*. A young doctor fixing the transmitter during Chen Yi's speech

Chen Yi's discourse over an empty landscape

for the wounded and the dead. Wen-ching and Hinoe are in the hallway, waiting for Hinomi. When she appears, Chen Yi's voice fades and we start hearing the hushed tones of the conversation between the young woman and the two men. The soundtrack quickly overlays Hinomi's voice as she reads from her diary: 'The radio today reported an incident in Taipei … Taipei is under martial law … A war has ended, how can another start again? Brother came to the hospital to see me. He's going to Taipei with Wen-ching …' Hinomi's voice continues over the next shot, in which we see her writing her diary.

A cut brings us to a room, drowned in darkness, at night, only lit by the shape of a window overlooking a dimly lit street; noises and commotion are heard outside; a woman arrives from the left on the screen, and, seen only in silhouette from the back, stands in front of the window, then opens it, and slightly bends down. We hear the coarse, throaty cry of a man. The woman turns her head back and we recognise Hinomi. The next shot is, again, of the hospital entrance, with people hurriedly coming and going, bringing the wounded, sometimes accompanied by their frightened relatives, and carrying torches. Chen Yi's second speech starts over this shot, announcing 'lenient measures'. It is then followed by a view of the hospital staff listening to the rest of his speech, gathered around the radio in their office, around a desk lamp; the material source of the speech is stressed, as static noises interfere briefly with the broadcast, and one of the doctors fixes the problem by tuning the receiver. Another cut brings us back to the hospital entrance, the same night, as the speech continues, promising a series of pacifying measures.

Meanwhile, the nurses comfort the relatives of the wounded. A close-up allows us to identify Wen-ching crouching in the doorway, with dark circles around his eyes, scribbling feverishly. Hinomi walks in, alarmed, asks him what he's doing there, and there is a hurried exchange of written notes before the young man faints.

Another speech by the governor starts over a quiet landscape, with a single, thick electric wire crossing the sky: 'Yesterday temporary Martial Law was again pronounced. I am here to emphasize with 120% sincerity [sic] to peace-loving people that my announcement of the Martial Law is totally for your protection.' The speech is carried over the next image: Hinomi knocks at the upper glass panel of Wen-ching's house. The photographer's assistant ushers her in and the governor's words fade out as she rushes upstairs to meet Wen-ching, asking him, first vocally, then in writing, where her brother is, which triggers another exchange of written notes ('Hinoe is safe … many people have died in Taipei …') and then a flashback in which the young man recounts being harassed and almost seriously beaten in the train by native Taiwanese who had mistaken him for a mainlander, because of his inability to speak either Taiwanese or Japanese. The report of such a small incident (compared to the magnitude of the massacre) *through the narration of a deaf-mute protagonist* is another subtle way Hou sets a tension between the official, clamouring, *acousmatic* voices of the official history and the intimate tragedies that are anchored in the individual bodies of private citizens. Yet it is highly significant that the *only male narrator is mute*. His handicap, as well as his intellectual tastes and artistic profession, somehow 'feminises' Wen-ching, turning him into a silent, reflexive observer – the counterpoint of Hinomi.

Hinomi is first introduced as an *acousmêtre*. Her voice is heard over the shot of a mountain landscape in which men carrying a sedan chair are seen at a distance. As they are approaching, the figure, then the face of the young woman on the chair become clear. At this moment, she is silent, her lips are not moving but, from what is said on the soundtrack, we are able to identify the voice as being *hers*, through a process that Chion calls *visualisation*.[58] This visualisation, though, is imperfect, as there is a discrepancy between the moment Hinomi appears on the screen and the moment her words are articulated. It is also a convention of narrative cinema, as the *utterances* of such voice-overs are fictional: they are the private, silent thoughts of the protagonist commenting on the action or writing a diary or a letter. Hinomi completely stops being an *acousmêtre* when she speaks in sync. However, as we are gently seduced by her soothing voice, which guides us through the narration of *A City*, we tend to overlook an important point: *Hinomi rarely speaks in sync.* The first line she utters ('photographs?') is addressed to the deaf Wen-ching and the second instance of her speech takes place during her encounter with Shisuko. When around men who can hear her she is mostly a silent observer, except for a few dramatic outbursts ('Doctor! Quick!'). For Hinomi, speech is the locus of private emotion (whenever she speaks to Wen-ching, it is because she is upset and/or frustrated), of exchange among women, of reflection. We never see an action initiated or changed by anything Hinomi says – while, in the world of men, killing, smuggling and politicking always generate a lot of talk. When Hinomi acts on her desire (leaving her family after her father 'grounds' her, and regularly visiting the Lin house), it happens either off-screen or in silence.

Cinematically and diegetically, Hinomi is 'on the edge', both *within and without* (a situation that can be connected to the way Lacan defines the situation of woman in relation to the symbolic order as 'not wholly in').[59] As an *acousmatic voice*, she is somewhat external to the screen image, above which she is 'floating'. As a non-member of the Lin family during most of the film, she can only watch what is happening to them. For Hou,

Hinomi plays the role of an observer. It allowed me to create an ambiguity in the narrative structure which I found very exciting – how the whole story is told from the point of view of a woman, who reports the events while expressing her emotions – a point of view that is both objective and subjective.[60]

This phrase expresses one of the powerful paradoxes of Hou's work. On the one hand, it falls completely within the parameters of what Deleuze defines as 'modern cinema', in which 'the distinction between subjective and objective tends to lose its importance … We run in fact into a principle of indeterminability, indiscernibility: we no longer know what is imaginary or real, physical or mental.'[61] *On the other hand*, the opposition between subjective and objective plays a major role in Chinese traditional aesthetics, in which 'pure art is subjective, whereas narrative is objective'.[62] So, to become 'pure art', a narrative film needs a female narrator (which casts a new light on Hou's collaboration with Chu Tien-wen). Similarly, without women, Chinese society would be pure violence, pure exteriority:

A woman accepts what is happening outside – silently. Yet this is how woman becomes the really strong persistent force in the Chinese family. This is what I wanted to show by staging so many eating rituals, in which we see men eating and women standing on the side, taking care of domestic affairs, of the kids.[63]

Since, for Hou, women are prone to express the emotions experienced by an entire society, the narration *had to* be carried by female voices to create a 'subjective feeling' of the time. Women are the backbone of the Chinese family, which they hold together *from the inside* as the primeval Nü Wa was holding the vault of heaven. And, as in any classical kinship structure, women represent a mode of exchange between men. Such is the role played by Big Brother Wen-heung's mistress between her brother Ah-ga and the males of the Lin family; by Shisuko between her brother and Hinoe; by Hinomi between Hinoe and Wen-ching; and finally by Ah-shue, Wen-heung's older daughter, between her favourite uncle, Wen-ching, and his intellectual friends on the one hand, and the rest of the Lin family on the other. So, while Ah-shue's screen presence was eventually reduced at the editing stage,[64] she retains her structural importance by being, in her epistolary exchange with Hinomi, one of the two narrative vectors carrying the film to its conclusion.

As the protagonists only have fragmented visions of the reality as it unfolds, Hou eschews the omniscient voice-over commentary as it is played in film noir, for example. In later films, Hou explores a more classical use of the voice-over – that of Liang Ching in *Good Men, Good Women*, and an anonymous female voice in *Millennium Mambo*. This recent evolution renders the status of the voice-over in his work more mysterious. In both *A City* and *Good Men*, the speakers are eventually identifiable *within the genesis*; it is no longer the case in *Millennium Mambo*. Leo Ou-fan Lee argues that the structural use of the voice-over in Hou's work is comparable to that of Wong Kar-wai's – both are a trope inherited from Chinese literature, a way of expressing interiority in its relationship to time.[65] In Wong's *Chungking Express*, it is impossible to decide if the voice-over describes an event *at the moment it is taking place* or *the nostalgia of a moment that has already fled*. In *A City*, Hou experiments with temporal shifts in relation to the voice-over – that happens sometimes after, and sometimes before or during the action it comments upon. The experiment is conducted further with the multiple temporalities (no fewer than five) that overlap in *Good Men, Good Women*, and reaches another level of complexity in *Millennium Mambo*, where the 'voice', which is *speaking several decades later after the events staged on-screen*, is constantly out of phase with their representation.

Similarly, discussing the relationship between Hou and Ozu, the Japanese film historian Shiguehiko Hasumi argues that the 'practical lesson bequeathed [by] Ozu's cinema [to Hou is] the research of a lost present'.[66] Due to the particular historical circumstances of Taiwan and the exile of Hou's family, the present was foreclosed for Hou, while Ozu significantly avoided films taking place in the past:

an absence ... that deepened [Hou's] nostalgia for the present. One has the feeling that [Hou and Ozu] were two directors having ... found comparable cinematic solutions, one because he was trapped in the present, and the other because he is trapped in the past.[67]

Hou's use of the voice-over exemplifies this acute feeling that the present is always what-is-missing, for it flees before we have time to experience it. The voice remains, resonating over an empty shot …

4 Lost Spaces

While indebted to Hasumi's original reformulation of the convergence between Ozu's and Hou's *perception of time*, we cannot ignore the issue of possible influences on Hou's spectacular visual compositions. Hou explains the genesis of his directing style as a reaction against the practices prevailing in Taiwanese commercial cinema.

The shooting ration was about 3 to 1. To save film stock, they were forcing us to do a detailed breakdown. It was very difficult for the actors, because they were not acting in a 'real' situation, but, were, for example, talking to a fist off-camera. When I became a director, I thought 'why don't we let them complete the whole conversation in one take?' It made me rethink the ethics of every shot. And I found long takes to be much more exciting to do than short cuts or close-ups …[68]

Still a work of transition, *A City* contains a number of medium shots – a practice discarded in the film that immediately follows it, *The Puppetmaster*. However, the tropes of Hou's now eminently recognisable *mise en scène* are already there: one-shot sequences that explore both duration and the depth of space; elliptic editing and compositions that function as tableaux, or, even better, 'blocks' of discontinuous time/space; 180° reverse-angle cuts; the recurrence of empty spaces; a fondness for putting the camera at a distance – especially for scenes of violence, represented in extreme long shots. Human activity is not what commands the framing. In domestic scenes, people keep entering and leaving the frame, not only from the right and the left of the screen, but from the back of the space, or from an off-screen area located beyond the 'fourth wall'. Children are running around in all directions, pots are carried from the kitchen to the dining table, visitors arrive … In sequences that take place in the countryside, Hou frequently leaves the protagonists to embrace a vision of nature.

A distinctive feature of *A City* is the presence of what I have called visual motif shots (because of their rhythmical, almost musical, repetitive quality) – a feature Hou had already inserted in his previous film, *Daughter of the Nile*. The first of these shots concludes the 'birth sequence' at the beginning of *A City*. It's an extreme long shot of a landscape at night – with black and grey mountains overlooking some expanse of water and drowned in mist – a classical visual trope. 'The misty monochrome landscape represents for many the culmination of hundreds of years of Chinese paintings.'[69] This particular image recurs five times throughout the film, and it is the first of a series of repetitive shots that show a location *with the same or a similar angle* but at different moments of the narration. The striking composition of this landscape, totally devoid of human presence, sets it apart from the three other most important visual motif shots: the entrance of the hospital where Hinomi works, the street leading to a nightclub and a

Visual motif shot of the street leading to 'Little Shanghai'

view of the Lin family dining room (all of these are places where people keep coming and going, except in the much-written-about last, empty shot of the film). Assessing the similarities and differences between Hou's visual motif shots and Ozu's *pillow shots* is complex. Noel Burch describes pillow shots – a term he coined – as a 'very particular use of "cutaway-still-life" … [that] *suspends the diegetic flow*, using a considerable range of strategies and producing a variety of complex relationships'.[70] Ozu's pillow shots are still life – the flower vase in *Late Spring* (1949) for example. Conversely, one of the most often used visual motif shots in *A City* – the entrance to the Miners' Hospital – is the site of intense human activity.

However, I will argue that a decentring effect of a similar order to the one produced by the pillow shots functions in Hou's visual motif shots

– whether or not there are people in them. Their composition is ordered by a (usually) fixed camera, filming frontally, removed from the action it records, whose framing strategy mixes the rigour of following the lines of the architecture or the landscape and the apparent nonchalance of letting human activity 'escape' its confines. This has multiple effects that unfold, *in time* and often *retroactively*, in the mind of the viewer. First it seems as if people are filmed like still life objects; like the diamond-shaped stained glass, the table, the doorway, the mountain, they are part of the setting, of the landscape. On second thought, one realises how *transitory* and *accidental* the human presence is. Unlike the stained glass, the table, the doorway, the mountain, which remain in the shot even when 'nothing happens' or after most of the protagonists are dead, people are floating over the composition of the shot like unnecessary ghosts. The shot does not need them. And they do not need the shot either. For a *third* meaning slowly emerges from our reflection. As people keep coming and going in and out of the frame, cooking, chatting, gambling, tending the wounded, casting off-screen glances, reacting to noises or actions that are taking place off-screen as well, they appear to be completely free to wander. No third assistant is yelling at them to 'keep their marks'. *A City* admits very few reverse-angle shots to suture their vision or follow them when they have left the frame. There is an implicit *resistance* on the part of these bodies who exist, indulge in everyday, mundane activities, without paying attention to the organisation of the shot. They are both ghost-like (and unnecessary) and mineral (and permanent). In Taiwan, women were washing, cooking and tending children, men were gambling, arguing and fighting way before the invention of the camera and they will do so long after this cumbersome apparatus is reduced to rubble.

A similar freedom is granted the spectator, as his/her gaze is free to wander within the shot as well, since no hierarchy is established between background and foreground, centre and edges, figures and setting. This is particularly true of the visual motif shots. Like in music the use of a repetitive form frees the mind from contemplating, after the second and third occurrence, the *structuring design*, and makes it possible instead to focus on minute, subtle details – a woman singing, the gradation of lights, a small gesture. Moreover, Burch's analysis implies that the *decentring effect* produced by the pillow shots comes not so much from their being 'unpeopled', but from the fact that their focal point is not the human figure: 'fully articulated from the graphic point of view, they demand to be *scanned* like paintings',[71] a description that applies to Hou's compositions as well.

So – what is the level of Ozu's influence over Hou? One must first consider how Hou has arrived at the tropes that compose his cinema. From the onset, even in his most commercial productions, there is a desire to translate the Taiwanese space onto the silver screen. It is a space that, for all its elegiac beauty, was fragmented, contradictory, foreclosed. For the immigrant mainlanders, like the protagonist's grandmother in *The Time to Live* who kept hoping that if she walked far enough she would get back 'home', it was the imperfect shadow image of the land that had been lost. For the native Taiwanese, it was a space that had been twice taken away from them, onto which occupying forces had attempted to rewrite history, by imposing their architecture, their political system, their language; it was a space marked by blood, jails, silence and repression. For those who, like Hou, grew up there in the 1950s and 1960s, it was the contained, yet exciting space of their coming of age, in which the younger generation accumulated experiences that differed from their parents' experiences – from the macho bonding of grass-roots delinquency to the lures, wonders and anxiety of an approaching modernity. For all – especially during the diplomatic isolation of the 1970s – it was a place you could not leave. The mainland was closed off; Japan was no longer the colonising power; only rich boys could hope to study abroad, and even in their case, only after completing two or three years' military service. The only thing to do was to work really hard – and this is what produced the 'Taiwan economic miracle' of the 1970s, with its assorted human catastrophes of rural exodus, displacement, destruction of natural resources, huge pockets of poverty in inflated urban centres … It was a dislocated space.

The sophisticated, elegant lines of Japanese architecture that are at the centre of Ozu's cinematic language allowed him to reclaim an undisturbed Japanese space. On the other hand, when such architecture appears in a Taiwanese film, its meaning is at once bifurcated: upper class gentility, nobility, style *and* the mark of years of occupation. For Hou, the connection between his protagonists and the land *bypasses* architecture in order to go through the landscape – this ambiguous, in-between space that is, however, the only possibility for mooring. The design of 'the Taiwanese trilogy' is site-specific even if, at every turn, we're faced with 'lost space'. To shoot *A City*, Hou used a *former* mining town, a place that had *outlived* its usefulness and was surviving its own history.

Gilles Deleuze stresses that the 'empty, disconnected spaces' of *modern* cinema command a new *reading* of the visual image (hence a different involvement of the spectator) and an alternative editing strategy:

An empty space, without characters (or in which the characters themselves show the void) has a fullness in which nothing is missing. Disconnected, unlinked fragments of space are the object of a specific relinkage over the gap: the absence of match is only the appearance of a linking-up which can take place in an infinite number of ways.[72]

The diegetic space of *A City* is both impressionist and fragmented. In any given location, Hou 'likes only one or two camera angles'[73] – disregarding establishing shots through which the spectator could find his/her bearings, as well as reverse-angle editing that would allow identification – and often cuts at an 180° reverse angle. As a result, it is almost impossible for the spectator to reconstruct the space. The relationship between different areas of the same house is not given through classical *découpage,* but *through the soundtrack*: in the kitchen, the women are hearing the faint noise of the musicians playing in the main room, giving a vague idea of their proximity to the social gathering. When a given space is fragmented or 'de-composed', it is through a concertina (that usually goes from a close-up or medium shot to a long shot): the angle of vision is not changed, but the spatial relationships between objects and people are.

The feeling of being 'lost' is furthered by Hou's nonchalant disregard of continuity rules at the editing table. For example, he discarded a sequence showing Big Brother Wen-heung escaping from the roof of his mistress's house when Kuomintang's agents seek to arrest him.

Instead, he cut to a shot of the Lin family house, in which Grand-Pa Lin is copiously insulting the soldiers. It takes repeated viewings to understand that the bulk of the narration takes place between two different towns: the port of Baduzi (where the Lin family lives and does business) and the mountain town of Chiu-fen (home of Hinoe, Wen-ching and Hinomi).

In the two other films of 'the Taiwanese trilogy', Hou was to expand his filmic vocabulary to keep exploring the trope of 'lost space'. *The Puppetmaster*, which recounts the years of Japanese occupation through the wanderings of Li Tien-lu throughout the island, posed a specific problem: because of Taiwan's pervasive industrialisation, it was impossible to find villages and landscapes in a state remotely approaching what they looked like 50 years before. So, benefiting from the lifting of the ban on travel to mainland China, Hou shot a great part of the film in the coastal province of Fujian, which is less developed than the rest of the country.[74] In addition, Hou went further in a systematic setting of shots-as-tableaux, creating striking, large-scale compositions that admitted no reverse angle and that no close-up or medium shot came to break down. *Good Men, Good Women* adds a new level of poignancy to the feeling of loss. The heroine, Liang Ching, exists simultaneously in several temporalities – her own past as a bar hostess/drug addict/gangster moll, her present as a struggling young actress who seeks oblivion in promiscuous love affairs, and the film role she's rehearsing, of a young leftist intellectual victim of the White Terror in the 1950s. Nowhere is Ching 'home' – a feeling of anxiety pervades a permanently decentred image, as if 'what is essential' was always out of her sight, out of her reach. And the images of the present, the banal, neon-lit, urbanised Taiwan are haunted by the hidden memories of the past, which Ching's involvement in cinema brings back to the surface. The historical character she plays, Chiang Bi-yu, is also constantly displaced, as proven by a poignant scene in which she and her companions, having enthusiastically arrived on the mainland to join the Communist partisans in their anti-Japanese fight, are caught in another linguistic imbroglio (the mainlanders only speak Cantonese) and almost shot as Japanese spies! Back home, having 'won' on the anti-Japanese front, they are immediately suspected, unwanted and finally persecuted as

Communist sympathisers. The ultimate sadness in Hou's 'Taiwan trilogy' lies in this ambiguous message: his characters are floating over Taiwan like the voice-over in his films – with an essential but tenuous connection, under the permanent threat of their own erasure.

Hou and Traditional Chinese Aesthetics

In the opening shot of *Good Men, Good Women*, an elegant camera movement sweeps through the apartment of the heroine and reveals a TV screen, where one can recognise images from the bicycle trip sequence in Ozu's *Late Spring*. 'The actress is about to play the role of a woman living in the 1950s,' explains Hou. 'The director has advised her to watch this film, that belongs to the imaginary world she must absorb to get into her character.'[75] Yet – why Ozu rather than a master of Chinese cinema of the 1940s and 1950s? According to Hasumi, 'when Hou became a director, he had seen none of the films of the Japanese master. He discovered Ozu at the end of the 1980s … when he was already the author of seven feature films, during a visit to France that coincided with the French release of Ozu's silent film, *I Was Born, But …* (1932) that immediately seduced him and remains his favourite movie.'[76] Rather than of *influence*, we should talk about *convergence*, and investigate traditional Chinese and Japanese aesthetics as a source of inspiration for both Ozu and Hou …

In Japan and China, classical landscape painting developed along principles radically opposed to the Renaissance perspective and the techniques of 'realistic' lighting and chiaroscuro used by Western painters. The relationship between foreground and background, background and figure follows a different philosophical order. Rather than being structured from a fixed viewpoint (the 'master gaze' of the observer) commanding vanishing points and different layers of depth that are perceived *simultaneously*, the landscape painting unfolds a flat space that demands to be read from multiple perspectives; 'reading' a painting is a process that takes place in time, as the viewer, leisurely, goes 'from top to centre, then from centre to bottom, thus proceeding from distant to near at hand'[77] in a process that parallels the meditative walk of the scholar through a landscaped garden.[78] Not surprisingly, Chinese aesthetics consider painting and calligraphy as two branches of the same art. The lack of a master gaze, the painterly compositions, the pure play of surfaces unfolding without being sutured by a reverse-angle shot, the meditative length of the one-shot sequences that characterise Hou's cinema are clearly a way of negotiating the heritage of classical Chinese painting into his work.

In the case of a national cinema with a strong visual/narrative tradition completely independent from Western aesthetics, such negotiation is neither obvious nor easy. Introduced in a context of physical or symbolic violence (colonialism, imperialist wars), as an element of the 'forced' entry of modernity into a traditional culture, and later part and parcel of a bitter economic competition with American cinema, cinema often behaves like a Trojan horse: seducing the audience, it also contributes to the destruction of indigenous values. In a Chinese cosmopolitan city like Shanghai, early cinema successfully negotiated a merging of traditional aesthetics with a filmic vocabulary learnt from American cinema (a negotiation similarly achieved by early Japanese cinema). Conversely, a dominated, dislocated film industry like that of Taiwan found it much more difficult to 'find its voice'. There is an essential contradiction between cinema and the Chinese pictorial tradition: on the one hand, the camera apparatus is designed according to the principles of Renaissance perspective; on the other, the framing of image parallels that of the Western painting – while the boundaries of the Chinese scroll are, theoretically, 'limitless'. So, in Hou's practice as a film-maker, this tradition, far from being a given, was lost in the 'rules' of the Taiwanese film industry, and could only be reached as a sort of *return of the repressed* that took years to achieve. Hou's interest in restoring this tradition matches his effort to bring to light hidden aspects of Taiwanese history.

Yet what is lost is never to be regained in its original form, and for Hou the act of reclamation was a process conducted in permanent dialogue with the West. When Hou was preparing *The Boys from Fengkuei*, Edward Yang lent him a tape of Pasolini's *Oedipus Rex* (1967), which made him discover what Deleuze calls the *'free indirect discourse'*: the image is neither subjective nor objective, it corresponds neither to a direct discourse nor to an indirect discourse ... it is rather a case of an assemblage of enunciation, carrying out two inseparable acts of subjectivation simultaneously, one of which constitutes a character in the first person, but the other of which is present at his birth and bring him to the stage (le mettant en scène).[79]

At the same time, Godard's *Breathless* (1960) impressed him for his destruction of the classical system by 'editing together long shots, medium shots and close-ups: he simply films emotions, independently of the size of the shots'.[80] So, even though Hou proudly claims that he's 'inscribed in perfect continuity with ancient Chinese culture',[81] such inscription happens *after the fact*, achieved through the work itself that embodies both a hard-won cultural specificity *and* the tropes of the most modern forms of contemporary cinema.

As Lacan points out, within the system of Renaissance perspective, 'the subject is caught, manipulated, captured in the field of vision'. The vanishing point without which there is no depth of field functions as a signifier of the place of the subject: 'I am not simply this punctiform being located at the geometral point from which perspective is grasped ... The picture, certainly, is in my eye. But *I* am in the picture.'[82] The Renaissance perspective is a double-entry mechanism: projecting the object *out* in the field of vision of the spectator and introjecting the spectator *into* the painting or the screen. As classical Chinese painting relies on a system of representation that eschews suture and perspective, it expresses the subjectivity of both the artist and the spectator through the dialectic between form and emptiness. For François Cheng, the Void, a central concern in Chinese thought,

makes possible the interaction, even the transmutation between Heaven and Earth, and, consequently, between Space and Time. As Time is perceived as an actualisation of the Vital Space, the Void, by reintroducing discontinuity within the unfolding of time, re-injects some of the quality of Space into time.[83]

The goal of a Chinese painting is *not* to represent reality as it appears to the naked eye, but to manifest the true essence of things. In some paintings, 'the Void (non painted spaces) represents up to two thirds of the canvas … Even an innocent spectator feels that the Void is not an inert presence but … connects the visible world to an invisible one.'[84] By inserting large amounts of blank space into his landscapes, the painter brings to light his subjective vision to capture the *invisible essence of things as they are filtered through his emotions or his memories*. The blank spaces, thus, play the same role in Chinese art as the vanishing points in Renaissance paintings: they mark the place of the subject.

It is within this dialectic between the 'objective' aspect of narrative cinema and the 'subjective' quality of art that one can read Hou's use of empty spaces: he displays them as subjective scansions, to 'create, or to expand emotions'.[85] Some of his most beautiful images are long tracking-sequence shots showing a character journeying through a bucolic landscape, a deserted road: Hinomi being carried on a sedan to start her new life; Wen-ching going to visit Hinoe in his guerrilla camp. In elegant sweeping motions, the camera follows the protagonists, then loses them at the turn of the road and lingers on an unspoilt sight of nature (mountains, rice paddies …). Here Hou plays a subtle balancing act with the tropes of narrative cinema (a character is going from A to B, with something to do) and the subjective, elegiac tone of traditional Chinese art (moments of contemplation in front of a landscape).

In Chinese, the word landscape is made of two characters: mountain/water – they summarise the universe, as a dialectic between opposites that is made possible *only through the presence of the Void*, which allows mountain to become water and vice versa. This is why clouds, or mist, play such an important role in the representation. In *A City*, Hou plays a series of variations on the classical notion of landscape – starting with the first visual motif shot of mountains overlooking the sea and drowned in mist. Yet, as a *modern* film-maker, he brings pure cinematic devices to explore the notion of empty space. In one of the last occurrences of this shot, which precedes Big Brother Wen-heung's funeral, he uses a slow camera movement, from right to left, to energise and bring tension into this image. The camera at first seems to follow the evolutions of a blackbird, which flies over the mountains, and then, as the bird starts

Visual motif shot of the landscape in
daylight

Long shot of the harbour at night

circling over, leisurely, the movement of the camera and those of the bird
become disconnected, introducing in the image, through this subtle
discrepancy, a figure of the 'Void'.

At the end of the film, Hou produces his 'modernist' version of a
traditional landscape soiled by industrialisation and history. A flat
composition shows a tree on the right, distant mountains on the left and,
in the background, a vast expanse of water, over which a blank, empty sky
is looming. The disjunctive elements are not, here, a bird and a camera
movement, but a rather ugly wooden fence that crosses the frame, slightly
obliquely, and below it, rail tracks. The sound of an approaching train is
heard. There is a disorienting cut (repeated viewings have not helped me
find out if this was an 180° cut or simply another space) leading to a more
tightly framed image. We see – behind a passing train that functions, if not
like a mist, at least like a veiling, distancing device – Wen-ching, Hinomi
and their baby, standing on the platform. When the train leaves, we get a
better view: the tree is still on the right, the water in the background,

partially blocked by the wooden fence, but the mountains are no longer in the frame, as if, by crossing the image, in its cumbersome and noisy uselessness (the protagonists having decided that fleeing was no longer an option), it had destroyed the fabric of the landscape, introducing a new type of Void. Moreover, the train slices through the flat image, splitting it into two layers that create an illusory depth – *for there is nobody to look at it*. Wen-ching and his family are gazing through the forbidding, dark surface of the cars as they pass, and once the train is gone, they gaze at something we cannot see (no reverse angle here). The passing of the train symbolises *nothing* – neither the possibility to leave, nor that of suturing one's gaze.

The Void becomes a recurring figure in Hou's *cinematic language itself*, particularly in his use of the voice-over and the intertitles of the written exchange between Wen-ching and Hinomi. While some have described such devices as 'unfilmic',[86] they create a dialogue between visual image, silence and sound, giving the latter its autonomy by inserting 'a fault, an interstice, an irrational cut between … the visual image and the sound-image' in which Deleuze sees one of the cornerstones of modernity.[87] Furthermore, Hou's use of intertitles is also a return to some of the tropes of early cinema (another modernist stance) while integrating another pole of his artistic inspiration – the traditional presence of calligraphy in Chinese painting.

The arc-light trajectory of the film also rests on Hou's dialectic between 'fullness' and 'emptiness'. At the beginning, out of a dark house, without electricity, a life is born, and light returns. At the end, one of the most-used visual motif shots – the Lin family dining room, with its bright lozenge-shaped stained glass – is finally emptied of human presence, and becomes, for our captivated gaze, an alluring and tragic figure of the Void.

5 An Aesthetic of the Fleeting Moment

In the last 13 minutes of *A City of Sadness*, the soundtrack is interrupted only twice, and the image unfolds through a series of 13 shots. I will start the description of the sequence at the end of a long shot, in which Hinomi writes her diary on the kitchen table. Off-screen, her infant son, Ah-chien, prattles. The first interruption of the soundtrack brings us to another time and space – from the quiet, luminous space of the kitchen to the threats and sorrows of the night.

We jump to a dark hallway; while a knock is heard on the door, and a dog is barking outside. Wen-ching admits someone who gives him a letter.

In the couple's bedroom, Hinomi feeds the baby from a bowl. Wen-ching walks in, turns on the light, gives his wife the letter and sits down. She reads it, remains motionless, then slowly resumes, almost mechanically, to feed the baby. The baby plays with the letter, which Hinomi eventually retrieves. She cries. Her husband takes her hand. They hug. The shot lasts long enough (almost two minutes) for a momentum to be created – a method often used by Hou, especially in moments of sorrow. A tension is created through the contrast between Tony Leung's superb professional acting, the way Hsin Shu-fen reaches an emotional plateau and ends up shedding real tears, and the baby's playful, innocent, unaware non-acting. At the end of the shot, the soundtrack of the next sequence overlaps the enclosed image of the little family, announcing the violence of what is about to follow (an explanation of the content of the letter).

The narrative flashback starts in the countryside, at night. The scene is shrouded in darkness, creating confusion. We see men being rounded up by other men carrying guns and shouting. A sharp order – 'Don't run!' – is followed by a gunshot. Then, the camera pans from left to right and remains on a deserted beach, as waves are gently lapping the shore.

The camera cuts to a tighter frame, to give us a closer look at the men kneeling down with their hands on their heads, as they are arrested by soldiers in uniform. A woman is brought outside, holding a crying baby.

The infant creates a striking parallel with Hinomi's and Weng-ching's son, seen earlier. The two children are cousins: we are witnessing the arrest of Hinoe and his comrades in their guerrilla camp. The second cut in the soundtrack occurs at the end of this shot.

The flashback is over, and we jump to a few days later, in a train station. A train approaches; Wen-ching and his family decide not to board it (see Chapter Four). The theme music starts in the middle of the second shot.

The music continues over a medium shot of Wen-ching, seen from the back, combing his hair in front of a mirror, adjusting his tie, etc. Off-screen, the baby prattles. Wen-ching takes his camera, turns around and looks intensely at the off-screen space, where we imagine his wife and baby to be. The music fades out. He puts the camera on a stool, and starts the remote control mechanism.

An 180° reverse angle reveals the 'scene' captured by the camera. Wen-ching and his family are sitting in the photography studio, with a conventional (Western-influenced) painted backdrop: flowers in a vase, fake window, fireplace.

As the camera clicks, the image freezes. The soundtrack is entirely silent. Here the clichéd device of the moving image frozen into a still photograph chillingly denotes the presence of death among the living. The picture thus taken will be enclosed in a letter, sent by Hinomi to Ah-shue, after Wen-ching's arrest. On the freeze frame, a female voice reads the letter, providing retrospective explanations for the images we have just seen: 'Fourth Uncle has been arrested. We still don't know where he is. Once we planned on leaving, but there is no way to escape.'

The voice continues while Ah-shue is reading the letter at the kitchen table: 'This photo was taken three days before your Fourth Uncle was arrested.'

The same female voice (now mixed with ambient sound) carries us to the next shot, the eighth occurrence of the visual motif shot of the Lin family's dining room – framed from a slightly different angle that presents mostly the left side of the room. At the table, Ah-ga, now the only valid man of the clan, is involved in a noisy game of mah-jong with a group of his gambling cronies, men and women, in sharp contrast with the elegiac tone of the letter: 'I have searched and enquired everywhere in Taipei, but I have no news. Ah-chien is growing teeth … His eyes are very much like your Fourth Uncle's … It is already growing cold in Chiu-fen; the reeds are in blossom.'

The letter-reading is over, but the ambient sound from the previous shot continues. Back in the kitchen, women are cooking – the only men present being Grand-Pa Lin and Wen-leung. Ah-ga walks in, picks up some food and returns to the dining room. The gambling and cooking are clearly improvised, providing a sort of documentary on Chinese culture, its rituals and internal space, *reclaimed* by Hou as a central trope in his cinema. At the end of the shot, percussion music starts.

The final image of *A City*, and also the most written about, is another visual motif shot of the dining room, with a return to the usual frame and angle, but *totally empty.* The theme music is heard while Chinese titles appear, suturing the feeling of loss and sadness towards which the movement of the entire film is directed: 'December 1949. The mainland was lost, the Nationalist government moved to Taiwan. And Taipei became the temporary capital.'[88]

Appendix 1: The Lin Family Genealogy

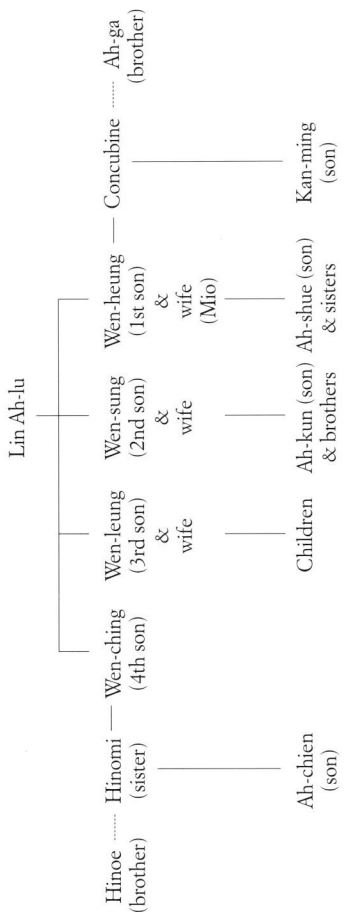

Lin Ah-lu

Hinoe ...... Hinomi — Wen-ching — Wen-leung — Wen-sung — Wen-heung — Concubine ...... Ah-ga
(brother)   (sister)   (4th son)   (3rd son)   (2nd son)   (1st son)   (brother)
                                      &   &   &
                                     wife   wife   wife
                                                              (Mio)

Ah-chien   Children   Ah-kun (son) Ah-shue (son)   Kan-ming
(son)   & brothers   & sisters   (son)

Appendix 2: Filmography

Hou Hsiao-hsien's Filmography

Cute Girl (*Jiu shi liuliu de ta*, 1980)

Cheerful Wind (*Feng'er titacai*, 1981)

Green, Green Grass of Home (*Zai na hepan qingcao qing*, 1982)

His Son's Big Doll (*Ezri de da wan'ou*, 1983) in the omnibus film *The Sandwich Man* (*Ezri de da wan'ou*); the two other episodes are Tseng Chuang-hsiang's *Vicky's Hat* (*Xiao Qi de nading maozi*) and Wan Jen's *The Taste of Apples* (*Pingguo de ziwei*)

The Boys from Fengkuei (*Fenggui lai de ren*, 1983)

A Summer at Grandpa's (*Dongdong de jiaji*, 1984)

The Time to Live and the Time to Die (*Tongnian Wangshi*, 1985)

Dust in the Wind (*Lianlian fengchen*, 1986)

Daughter of the Nile (*Niluohe nüer*, 1987)

A City of Sadness (*Beiqing chengshi*, 1989)

The Puppetmaster (*Ximeng Chensheng*, 1993)

Good Men, Good Women (*Haonan haonü*, 1995)

Goodbye South, Goodbye (*Zaijian, nanguo, zaijian*, 1996)

Flowers of Shanghai (*Hai Shang Hua*, 1998)

Millennium Mambo (*Quianxi Manbo*, 2001)

Chinese Films Cited

Cai Chusheng, *Song of the Fisherman* (*Yu Guang Qu*, 1934)

King Hu, *A Touch of Zen* (*Xia Nû*, 1971)

Edward Yang, *Floating Leaf/Floating Weeds* (*Fuping*, 1981), part of the TV series *11 Women* (*Shi yige nüren*)

In Our Times (*Qidai*, 1982) – four episodes directed by Edward Yang (*Wishes/Desires* [*Guanggyin de gushi*]), Chang Yi, Tao Dechen and Ko Yi-cheng

Chen Kuen-hou, *Growing Up* (*Xiao Bi de gushi*, 1983)

Edward Yang, *That Day on the Beach* (*Haitan de yi tian*, 1983)

Ling Zifeng, *Border Town* (*Biancheng*, 1984)

Edward Yang, *Taipei Story* (*Quinmei Zhuma*, 1985)

Stanley Kwan, *Love onto Waste* (*Dixia Qing*, 1986)

Derek Yee, *People's Hero* (*Renmin Yingxiong*, 1987)

Zhang Yimou, *Red Sorghum* (*Hong gaolian*, 1987)

Patrick Tam, *My Heart is that Eternal Rose* (*Shashou Hudie Meng*, 1988)

Stanley Kwan, *Full Moon in New York* (*Sange Nürende gushi*, aka *Ren Zai Niu Yue*, 1989)

Tsai Ming-liang, *Four Corners of the World* (*Hai Jiao Tian Ya*, 1989)

Wong Kar-wai, *Days of Being Wild* (*A fei zhengzhuan*, 1990)

John Woo, *A Bullet in the Head* (*Diexue Jietou*, 1990)

Zhang Yimou, *Raise the Red Lantern* (*Da hongdenglong gaogaogua*, 1991)

Edward Yang, *A Brighter Summer Day* (*Gulingjie shaonian sharen shijian*, 1991)

John Woo, *Hard Boiled* (*Lashou Shentan*, 1992)

Wong Kar-wai, *Chungking Express* (*Chongqing Senlin*, 1993)

Wong Kar-wai, *Ashes of Time* (*Dongxie XiDu*, 1994)

Wu Nien-jen, *A Borrowed Life* (*Duo-Sang*, 1994)

Wu Nien-jen, *Buddha Bless America* (*Tai Ping, Tian Guo*, 1996)

Edward Yang, *Mahjong* (*Maijiang*, 1996)

Wong Kar-wai, *Happy Together* (*Chunguang Zhaxie*, 1997)

Stanley Kwan, *Hold You Tight* (*Yuei kuaile, yue duolo*, 1998)

Edward Yang, *A One and a Two* (*Yi Yi*, 2000)

Wong Kar-wai, *In the Mood for Love* (*Huayang Nianhua*, 2000)

Notes

1 In 1935, Cai Chusheng's *Song of the Fisherman* (1934) received a prize at the Moscow Film Festival. In 1975, King Hu's *A Touch of Zen* (completed in 1971) received an award at Cannes. In 1988, Zhang Yimou's *Red Sorghum* won the Golden Bear in Berlin.
2 Kwan is a great admirer of Hou's work and years later, in *Hold You Tight* (1998), he paid homage to *A City* by showing a large poster of the film in the apartment of one of the protagonists.
3 Chiao Hsiung-ping (Peggy Chiao), 'The Camera-swept Back Alleys of History: An Interview with Hou Hsiao-hsien', in *China Times*, Taipei, 4–5 September 1989, quoted in June Yip, 'Constructing a Nation – Taiwanese History and the Films of Hou Hsiao-hsien', in *Transnational Chinese Cinemas: Identity, Nationhood, Gender*, ed. by Sheldon Hsiao-peng Liu (Honolulu: University of Hawaii Press, 1997), p. 162 n8.
4 Jonathan Rosenbaum, *Chicago Reader*.
5 Other critical studies describe *A City* as 'Hou's tenth film', as they are counting his 1983 short, *The Sandwich Man*.
6 Hou Hsiao-hsien, interview with the author, New York City, October 1989, trans. by Peggy Chiao (hereafter referred to as 'Hou interview, October 1989').
7 To my knowledge, the first English-language critic to have mentioned Impressionism in conjunction with Hou's work is J. Hoberman in his Spring 1987 *Village Voice* review of *Dust in the Wind* : 'Like paintings by Seurat and Monet [Hou's] films are less the imitation of life than its distillation.'
8 It should be noted that Mio only bore Wen-heung daughters, while his concubine gave him a son – an important consideration for a Chinese patriarch.

9 In my quotes from the film, I use the text of the English subtitles by Taiwanese film-maker Stan Lai in collaboration with Linda Jaivin for the version released abroad by Era International at the time of the Venice Film Festival. This version – called 'the international version' in my text – was shown at all film festivals demanding English subtitles. The subtitles made later for the video released in the UK by Artificial Eye are slightly different, and shorter. In many cases I have found the Lai/Jaivin subtitles to be more colourful, and also closer to the original spirit of the dialogue.
10 Yip identifies the protagonists' original Taiwanese names as Kuanrong and Kuanmei. Her transcription of Hinoe's and Hinomi's names ('Hiroe' and 'Hiromi') differs slightly from mine ('Constructing a Nation', p. 163 n15). I am reproducing the protagonists' names as they appear in the English subtitles and in the press material handed out at the Venice Film Festival.
11 In 1889, Japan became a constitutional monarchy. The Meiji restoration managed to preserve the basic structure of Japanese society, while eliminating the traditional class system and hereditary customs.
12 Chiang Kai-shek continued to focus on the anti-Communist fight rather than resisting the Japanese invasion. In 1936, when visiting the city of Xi'an, he was kidnapped by General Zhang Xueliang who wanted to force him to adopt an anti-Japanese stance. After two weeks of tense negotiations with Communist representatives, Chiang agreed to a united anti-Japanese front.
13 Nationalists (based in Chonqing) and Communists (based in Yan'an) never fought side by side. After the Japanese surrender Chiang was the United States only interlocutor.

14 The term signifies people of Chinese descent having arrived in Taiwan before 1949; the word 'aborigine' is used to designate the original inhabitants of the island.

15 Live narrator of silent movies – a practice that started with the first public screenings of the Lumière Brothers' and Edison's films in Japan in 1897, and continued till the advent of the talkies. In Taiwan, it was also used to comment on the action of Japanese films.

16 Founded in 1979, the Taipei Cinematheque has taken on the task of collecting, cataloguing and restoring these Taiwanese-language films.

17 Wu Nien-jen, interview with the author, Taipei, December 1989 – hereafter referred to as 'Wu interview, December 1989'.

18 Yang's episode (*Wishes/Desires*) was his second directorial job. The year before, he had contributed a feature-length episode, *Floating Leaf/Floating Weeds* to the TV series *11 Women* (1981).

19 Interviews with Hou by Olivier Assayas for his film, *HHH: Portrait of Hou Hsiao-hsien* (1997) – hereafter referred to as 'Assayas, Hou interview, 1997'; Emmanuel Burdeau, 'Rencontre avec Hou Hsiao-hsien', in *Hou Hsiao-hsien*, ed. by Jean-Michel Fredon (Paris: Cahiers du cinéma, 1999) – hereafter referred to as 'Hou interview, 1999', pp. 60–1.

20 Assayas, Hou interview, 1997.

21 A collection of Hwang's short stories (including 'His Son's Big Doll' and 'The Taste of Apples') has been published in English as Hwang Chun-Ming, *The Drowning of an Old Cat and Other Stories* (Bloomington: Indiana University Press, 1980).

22 Thomas B. Gold, 'Civil Society and Taiwan's Quest for Identity', in *Cultural Change in Postwar Taiwan*, ed. by Stevan Harrell and Huang Chün-chieh (Taipei: SMC Publishing, 1994), p. 61.

23 Wu interview, December 1989.

24 Born in Hong Kong, Tseng was a former documentary film-maker. Wan Jen was to become a major figure of the New Taiwanese Cinema.

25 Hou interview, October 1989.

26 Ibid.

27 Hou interview, 1999, p. 86. The spelling used in this interview is Giu Fen. Other sources indicate the *pinyin* transcription as Jiu-Fen, while in the subtitles of the film's international version, the town is identified as Chiu-fen.

28 Hou explains that he had 'shot *Dust in the Wind* not in the place where Wu Nien-jen had lived, for it had changed a lot since, but in Giu Fen, where later many scenes of *A City of Sadness* were shot' (Hou interview, 1999, p. 77). He specifies that he 'used to come to [Giu Fen] often before shooting *A City of Sadness* there. The gold mines had closed, the city was deserted, abandoned, the traces of the past were still visible. At the time of the gold mines, there were a lot of night clubs and girlie bars there. That place fit exactly what I was looking for' (Assayas, Hou interview, 1997). Part of the story is also supposed to take place in the small fishing port of Badouzi, but it was too modernised at that time, so the city of Jin-Gua-Shin was chosen as a 'stand-in'. These two cities and their mountains became famous in Taiwan after the release of the film, and later Edward Yang shot a sequence of *A Brighter Summer Day* (1991) there.

29 Assayas, Hou interview, 1997; Hou interview, 1999, p. 101.

30 Wu interview, December 1989.

31 Hou interview, 1999, p. 89; Yip, 'Constructing a Nation', p. 163 n14.

32 Taiwanese customs state that a wedding should take place either immediately (less than a month) after a funeral, or much later (one would have to wait a year).

33 Assayas, Hou interview, 1997.

34 Wu interview, December 1989.

35 'Hou Hsiao-hsien: Un Ciné Susurrante', in *Hou Hsiao-hsien*, ed. by Peio Aldazabal and Nieves Amieva (San Sebastian Film Festival, 1995), pp. 15–23. This text was adapted into part of *Nouvelles Chines, nouveaux cinémas* (Paris: Editions de l'Etoile, 1999), pp. 237–51.

36 The teahouse was eventually closed, and Hou now writes screenplays in the office of his production company.

37 Shen Congwen (1902–88) inspired many Chinese films, in particular the novella *Border Town*, later turned into a film of the same title by Ling Zifeng in 1984. Ignored on the mainland after 1949 for 'lacking political awareness' and banned for a while in Taiwan, Shen was 'rediscovered' in the 1980s – a phenomenon that has to be connected to the emergence of 'nativist literature'.

38 Hou interview, 1999, p. 73.

39 Hou interview, October 1989.

40 Assayas, Hou interview, 1997.

41 Chu Tien-wen, 'Les plus beaux films de Hou Hsiao-hsien', in Fredon (ed.), *Hou Hsiao-hsien*, p. 52.

42 Assayas, Hou interview, 1997.

43 See Stephen Teo, *Hong Kong Cinema*: *The Extra Dimension* (London: BFI, 1997), pp. 61–72. Wu Nien-jen said he was moved to direct his own autobiographical film, *A Borrowed Life*, by the fact that, in *Dust in the Wind*, Hou had not dealt with the relationship between father and son.

44 Chu, 'Les plus beaux films', p. 54.

45 See Marcel Granet, *La Pensée chinoise* (Paris: Albin Michel, 1968), pp. 101, 126; François Cheng, *Vide et plein*: *le langage pictural chinois* (Paris: Seuil, 1991).

46 Assayas, Hou interview, 1997.

47 Wu interview, December 1989.

48 Hou interview, October 1989.

49 Assayas, Hou interview, 1997.

50 Hou interview, October 1989.

51 Yip, 'Constructing a Nation', pp. 148–9.

52 Assayas, Hou interview, 1997.

53 http://cinemaspace.berkeley.edu/ Papers/CityOfSadness.

54 Lyrics by Miki Rofu and music by Yamada Kousaku.

55 The parallel with the fate of Hong Kong – 'leased' to the British Crown by the Qing, and then 'retroceded' to the PRC by the British–Sino agreement of 1984 – was clear to many artists and intellectuals in Hong Kong.

56 Nü Wa died exhausted by her efforts to mend the sky. See 'Mending Heaven', in Lu Xun, *Old Tales Retold* (1935; Beijing: Foreign Language Press, 1961), pp. 5–16.

57 Michel Chion, *La Voix au cinéma* (Paris: Editions de l'Etoile, 1982), pp. 25–33. This text is partially translated in the English version of another of Chion's texts, 'L'impossible mise-en-corps', translated as 'The Impossible Embodiment', in *Everything You Always Wanted to Know about Lacan … But Were Afraid to Ask Hitchcock*, ed. by Slavoj Žižek (London: Verso, 1992), pp. 195–207. See also Chion, *Audio-Vision*, ed. and trans. by Claudia Gorbman (New York: Columbia University Press, 1994), pp. 129–31.

58 Chion, 'The Impossible Embodiment', n1.

59 See Jacques Lacan, *Encore* (Paris: Le Seuil, 1975) – as well as a partial English translation in *Feminine Sexuality – Jacques Lacan and the école freudienne*, ed. and trans. by Juliet Mitchell and Jacqueline Rose (New York: W. W. Norton, 1983).

60 Hou interview, October 1989.

61 Gilles Deleuze, *Cinema 2: The Time-Image* (Minneapolis: University of Minnesota Press, 1989), p. 7.

62 Hao Dazheng, 'Chinese Visual Representation: Painting and Cinema', in *Cinematic Landscapes: Observations on the Visual Arts and Cinema of China and Japan*, ed. by Linda C. Ehrlich and David Desser (Austin: University of Texas Press, 1994), p. 60.

63 Hou interview, October 1989.

64 Ibid.

65 'On the Edge, Over the Edge: Hong Kong Cinema and Popular Culture', conference at the University of Wisconsin-Madison, 1–3 March 2001.

66 Shiguehiko Hasumi, 'Nostalgie du présent', in Fredon (ed.), *Hou Hsiao-hsien*, p. 50.

67 Ibid.

68 Hou interview, October 1989.

69 Douglas Wilkerson, 'Film and the Visual Arts in China: An Introduction', in Ehrlich and Desser (eds), *Cinematic Landscapes*, p. 42.

70 Noel Burch, *To the Distant Observer: Form and Meaning in the Japanese Cinema* (Berkeley: University of California Press, 1979), p. 160.

71 Ibid., p. 162.

72 Deleuze, *Cinema 2*, p. 245.

73 Hou interview, October 1989.

74 The PRC made the decision to halt the industrialisation of Fujian, because it was on the 'front line' and its installations could easily be damaged in case of an armed conflict with Taiwan.

75 Hou interview, 1999, p. 96.

76 Hasumi, 'Nostalgie du présent', p. 48.

77 Ni Zhen, 'Classical Chinese Painting and Cinematographic Signification', in Ehrlich and Desser (eds), *Cinematic Landscapes*, p. 67.

78 Hao Dazheng, 'Chinese Visual Representation, p. 52.

79 Deleuze, *Cinema 1: The Movement-Image* (Minneapolis: University of Minnesota Press, 1986), pp. 72–3. Hou says that the film inspired him to discover 'four different points of view in a film: the objective and subjective point of view of the director, and the objective and subjective point of view of the main protagonist' (Hou interview, 1999, p. 74).

80 Hou interview, 1999, p. 78.

81 Ibid., p. 79.

82 Jacques Lacan, *The Four Fundamental Concepts of Psychoanalysis* (New York: Norton, 1977), pp. 92, 96. I have corrected a mistake by the translator Alan Sheridan. While Lacan says 'Mais moi je suis dans le tableau', Sheridan writes 'But I am *not* in the picture.'

83 Cheng, *Vide et plein*, pp. 45, 67.

84 Ibid., p. 47.

85 Hou interview, October 1989.

86 Yip, 'Constructing a Nation', p. 146.

87 Deleuze, *Cinema 2*, p. 251.

88 An earlier version of this analysis appears as 'Three Asian Films: For a New Cinematic Language', *Cinematograph*, vol. 4 no. ??, 1990–1, pp. 133–6.

Credits

**BEIQING CHENGSHI/
A CITY OF SADNESS**

Taiwan, R.O.C.
1989
Production Companies
Era International presents
a 3-H Films production

Director
Hou Hsiao-hsien
Producer
Chiu Fu-sheng
Executive Producers
H. T. Jan
Michael Yang
Screenplay
Wu Nien-jen, Chu Tien-wen
Director of Photography
Chen Hwai-en
Editor
Liau Ching-sown

Music
Tachikawa Naoki
Music Performed by
Sens
Music Produced by
Tsai Tsun-nan, Funhouse
'Exile Trilogy' music by
Chen Jian-jong, Hsian Yu,
Lai Shi-wang
**Wedding Music
Performed by**
Yee Wan-ren Puppet
Theater
Ruantan Opera Instructor
Pan Yu-chiao
Sound Recordists
Du Du-jih, Yang Jinn-an
Associate Producer
Chang Hwa-kun
Art Directors
Liu Chih-hwa, Lin Tsun-wen
Lighting
Song Dian-sheng
Lighting Assistant
Cheng He-ping
Assistant Directors
George Chang,
Huang Jian-he,
Lin Ching-ying,
Chiu Juen-lung
Assistant Cameramen
Liu Chang-hou,
Wang Yung-ming,
Chang Da-lung,
Chiu Fa-chuen
Intertitle Photography
Liu Deguang De-kwong
Costumes
Chu Jin-wen

Unit Managers
Toa Jong-min, He Jinn-Ping,
Hsu Shih-jen,
Wu Jong-liang
Production Assistants
Wen Kuo-hsiung,
Din Hsiao-bei,
Hsu Shi-hsien,
Chang Hwa-kun
Continuity
Tsai Bong-he,
Chen Chun-hwa,
Li Chih-wei
Overseas Co-ordinator
Shu Kei
**Post-production
Co-ordination (Japan)**
Pia Co., Ltd
Japanese Translation
Chang Cheong-yin
Chen Chun-jen
**Subtitles for the
International Version**
Stan Lai, Linda Jaivin
Film Laboratory
Taipei Film Laboratory
Co., Ltd.
Tokyo Laboratory Ltd.
Recording Studio
AOI Studio Co. Ltd.
**Camera Equipment
Serviced by**
Arrow Cinematic Group

Cast
Tony Leung Chiu-wai
Lin Wen-ching
Hsin Shu-fen
Wu Hinomi
Chen Sown-yung
Lin Wen-heung
Kao Jai (AKA Jack Kao)
Lin Wen-leung
Li Tien-lu
Lin Ah-lu
Wu Yi-fang
Wu Hinoe
Huang Tsien-ru
Ah-shue
Nakamura Ikuyo
Shisuko
Kenny Cheung
Ah-ga
Chen Shu-fang
Mio, First Brother's wife
Ko Shu-yun
Second Brother's wife
Lin Li-ching
Third Brother's wife
Ko Ai-yun
First Brother's mistress
Law Chang-yeh
Ah-kun, First Brother's older
son
Lin Yang
Mr Ko
H. T. Jan
Mr Lin
Chen Yu-rung
Ah-tsun, Wen-ching's
assistant

Lin Juh
Kim-tsua, gangster
Ai Tsu-tu
'Red Monkey'
Ah Pi-poa
Ah-kio, lady arbitrator
Wu Nien-jen
Mr Wu
Chang Da-tsuen
Mr Ho
Hse Tsai-juen
Mr Hse
Lu Chin
Mr Wu, Hinomi's father
Mei Fang
Mrs Wu, Hinomi's mother
Lei Ming
Shanghai Boss
Lai De-nan
hospital administrator
Jin Shih-jeh
Mr Huang
Kao Jong-li
revolutionary
Chen Liang-yueh
army officer
Ma Wen-hou
Ruantan Opera singer
Nagatani Sentaro
Ogawa
Bi Li
Billy
Yan Chun-chun
nurse
Takakuwa Junko
Japanese woman

Duration
158 minutes
Format
1:1.85/35mm/Colour

Also Published

L'Argent
Kent Jones (1999)

Blade Runner
Scott Bukatman (1997)

Blue Velvet
Michael Atkinson (1997)

Caravaggio
Leo Bersani & Ulysse Dutoit
(1999)

Crash
Iain Sinclair (1999)

The Crying Game
Jane Giles (1997)

Dead Man
Jonathan Rosenbaum
(2000)

**Dilwale Dulhania Le
Jayenge**
Anupama Chopra (2002)

Don't Look Now
Mark Sanderson (1996)

Do the Right Thing
Ed Guerrero (2001)

Easy Rider
Lee Hill (1996)

The Exorcist
Mark Kermode (1997,
2nd edn 1998)

Eyes Wide Shut
Michel Chion (2002)

Heat
Nick James (2002)

Independence Day
Michael Rogin (1998)

Jaws
Antonia Quirke (2002)

Last Tango in Paris
David Thompson (1998)

**Once Upon a Time in
America**
Adrian Martin (1998)

Pulp Fiction
Dana Polan (2000)

The Right Stuff
Tom Charity (1997)

**Saló or The 120 Days of
Sodom**
Gary Indiana (2000)

Seven
Richard Dyer (1999)

The Silence of the Lambs
Yvonne Tasker (2002)

The Terminator
Sean French (1996)

Thelma & Louise
Marita Sturken (2000)

The Thing
Anne Billson (1997)

**The 'Three Colours'
Trilogy**
Geoff Andrew (1998)

Titanic
David M. Lubin (1999)

Trainspotting
Murray Smith (2002)

The Usual Suspects
Ernest Larsen (2002)

The Wings of the Dove
Robin Wood (1999)

**Women on the Verge of a
Nervous Breakdown**
Peter William Evans (1996)

**WR – Mysteries of the
Organism**
Raymond Durgnat (1999)

BFI MODERN CLASSICS

BFI Modern Classics combine careful research with high-quality writing about contemporary cinema.

If you would like to receive further information about future **BFI Modern Classics** or about other books from BFI Publishing, please fill in your name and address and return this card to us.*

(No stamp required if posted in the UK, Channel Islands, or Isle of Man.)

NAME

ADDRESS

POSTCODE

WHICH **BFI MODERN CLASSIC** DID YOU BUY?

* In USA and Canada, please return your card to:
University of California Press, 2120 Berkeley Way,
Berkeley, CA 94720 USA

BFI Publishing
21 Stephen Street
FREEPOST 7
LONDON
W1E 4AN